The Place of Criminal Justice in Developmental Planning

The book is published in conjunction with the United Nations

**Monographs of the
United Nations Crime Prevention
and Criminal Justice Section**

Dr. Kurt Neudek
General Editor

The Place of Criminal Justice in Developmental Planning

Hardy Wickwar

New York • New York University Press • 1977

Library of Congress Cataloging in Publication Data

Wickwar, William Hardy.
    The place of criminal justice in development planning.

    (Monographs of the United Nations Crime Prevention and
Criminal Justice Section ; v. 1)
    Published in conjunction with the United Nations.
    Includes bibliographical references.
        1.   Criminal justice, Administration of.   2.   Under-
developed areas—Criminal justice, Administration of.
I.   Title.   II.   Series: United Nations.   Crime
Prevention and Criminal Justice Section.   Monographs of
the United Nations Crime Prevention and Criminal Justice
Section ; v. 1.
HV8665.W45   364   76-16468
ISBN 0–8147–9170–0

Manufactured in the United States of America

Foreword

As part of its regular work program, the United Nations frequently commissions studies in the area of crime prevention and criminal justice. While the findings of these studies are usually United Nations official documents, the studies themselves have normally not been published. For some time, it has been felt that many of these studies deserve the attention of the entire community of scholars in the field of criminology, but so far there has been no provision for their independent publication. Pursuant to an agreement between the United Nations and New York University Press, a Monograph Series in Crime Prevention and Criminal Justice has now been inaugurated which makes such policy studies available to the scholarly community and the general public.

The present study is the first volume of the new series. It is devoted to a topic of particular significance to the United Nations work program, namely the place of criminal justice in development planning.

The relationship between unplanned development and increasing crime, which may nullify some of the hard-won gains of development, has been under consideration within the United Nations framework for some time. The Fourth and Fifth United Nations Congresses for the Prevention of Crime and the Treatment of Offenders, in 1970 and 1975 respectively, became both vantage points for reviewing and co-ordinating past endeavours and venues for formulating policy guidelines and programmes for action. Recommendations for criminal justice planning are also included in the United Nations international plan of action for crime prevention and control. This plan was finalized by the United Nations Committee on Crime Prevention and Control at its fourth session in June/July 1976. It will be submitted to the General Assembly in 1977 in pursuance of Assembly resolution 3021 (XXVII) of 18 December 1972.

Mr. Wickwar's study traces the directions which crime-related planning might take in order to reduce the negative consequences of crime and redistribute more easily and fairly consequences which are unavoidable. The author's considerations are based on the principle that the prevention and control of crime should be undertaken as a part of broad economic and social development planning. This principle has been endorsed by the United Nations Economic and Social Council in its resolution 1086 B (XXXIX) of 30 July 1965.

Criminal policy planning implies the existence of a unified approach to the analysis and planning of development, in which the economic and social approaches are fully integrated. National policies and plans can thus be formulated with a view to extending and ensuring human welfare and promoting desirable changes in social institutions and structures simultaneously with the achievement of the most tangible material objectives. Criminal policy planning should be understood as a process of socio-political transformation basically seeking a criminal justice that is social in nature. To the extent that criminal justice planning seeks to transform institutions, attitudes, conditions, and life-styles, it should not be limited simply to the reform of the present system of criminal justice.

While the planning process includes identification of goals, setting of targets, development of a general framework of strategy, allocation of resources, and monitoring of progress in implementation, other crucial factors of criminal justice planning are perhaps the most difficult to quantify and to control. These include adequate motivation and the optimization of social dynamics. Without these, the most rigorous cost/benefit analysis, ambitious planning or viable management scheme is an empty exercise. How to elicit the kind of motivation and foster a climate that promotes socially productive rather than destructive activity is one of the pivotal questions which social scientists, educators, national leaders, and ultimately society itself must resolve.

Gerhard O.W. Mueller
Chief
Crime Prevention and
Criminal Justice Section
United Nations

Contents

Introduction

The United Nations Economic and Social Council in 1965 endorsed "the principle that the prevention and control of juvenile delinquency and adult criminality should be undertaken as part of comprehensive economic and social development plans." (ECOSOC resolution 1086 B [XXXIX].)

This action by the Council represented an important milestone in the evolution of a new perspective on the phenomenon of criminality and on its prevention and control. It not only set the stage for critical analysis and logical planning nationally with respect to those services formally charged with the prevention and control of crime but, much more importantly, it alerted governments to the principle of viewing economic and social development objectives and methods in the light of their influence, positive or negative, on the nature and extent of criminality in the country.

For most countries, and in much international thinking, these approaches represented major departures. Understanding criminality and developing criminal justice systems were regarded essentially as tasks quite apart from national government goals and strategies. Indeed it was common, until relatively recently, to relegate the criminal justice field to "overhead" or "housekeeping" and to classify it as "nonproductive," thereby automatically excluding it from the developmental planning process.

With this very limited view of the criminal justice field, it was inevitable that the techniques of evaluation and planning fostered by central national planning authorities were seldom communicated to, or their application required of, the specialized services engaged in the prevention and control of crime. Indeed, in most instances where such sectoral planning has taken place, the initiative has come from within the field itself.

Limited as has been sectoral planning in the criminal justice field, an even greater gap has existed in comprehending broad economic and social development undertakings in relation to their potential for contributing to, or ameliorating, the social problems of juvenile delinquency and adult criminality. Obviously, no major economic or social development policy will be adopted or rejected on the sole basis of its impact on crime rates. Yet it is only logical that this factor be weighed realistically when all the pros and cons are being assessed.

Urban housing programs may contribute to lessening or aggravating problems of criminality, depending on how they are structured. Industrialization policies, rural-urban balance, centralization-decentralization of civil administration, orientation of primary and secondary education policy are seen to have great influence, for better or for worse, on patterns and volume of criminality. Still too little is understood about relationships of this nature. This is in large part because the relevance has been so little grasped that adequately mounted inquiries are infrequently conducted.

The United Nations, through its special publications, its *International Review of Criminal Policy*, its research and training institutes, and its technical meetings at the regional and international levels, has attempted to advance the aforementioned principle incorporated by the Economic and Social Council in its resolution 1086 B (XXXIX).

To build up the body of knowledge required to achieve the full inclusion of the prevention and control of juvenile delinquency and adult criminality as part of comprehensive economic and social development plans, certain basic steps were required. It was not even adequately known to what extent sectoral programs in this field were included in national development plans. Thus, when in 1971 the Council included in the social development work program "a survey of existing development plans to ascertain the extent to which social defense considerations are taken into account," the first objective was to catalogue and analyze those elements of national plans clearly identifiable as carrying sectoral responsibility for crime prevention and control. That is the scope of this report.

A subsequent undertaking must be an analysis of peripheral services identified as carrying recognized responsibility in the crime prevention and control field as, for example, child guidance and psychiatric programs. Ultimately, the more profound—and more complex—task will be to analyze the extent to which, and the means whereby, the crime-conducive or crime-preventive characteristics of developmental policies and programs are taken into consideration in the design and implementation of those programs.

This survey has been based on such national development plans as are available through the United Nations libraries and reference services. Although the collection is not complete (and not all the items in it have been available), there is every reason to believe that the hundred or so plans reviewed, of which about one half include provision for most aspects of crime control, are likely to constitute a representative sample.

The survey is concerned not with criminality as such but with governmental activity directed toward its containment; in other words, with known and measurable activity by such agents of government as the police, the courts, and the prisons.[1]

While it is focused primarily on the place of criminal policy in comprehensive development plans, it sometimes supplements

---

1. For a more detailed description of the method employed in this survey, see Appendix I.

data contained in a plan with budgetary and other official data throwing further light on dimensions of the government's criminal policy work load.

In view of the Council's interest in strengthening technical assistance for social defense through regional training, research, and advice, criminal policy has been analyzed region by region. To this has been prefixed a global synthesis or worldwide overview.

1

World Overview

A. RESOURCE ALLOCATION FOR CRIME CONTROL

In many developing countries, not only are developmental resources much scarcer than in developed countries but the proportion of the scarce resources available to government for allocation is also far smaller. It is therefore remarkable that resource allocation for crime control ranks exceedingly high among the priorities set by governments in developing countries.

1. THE REPORTED ORDER OF MAGNITUDE

This generalization concerning the high status frequently accorded to crime control in developing countries is equally valid whether the resources are human or fiscal.

Human resources: the proportion of manpower to total population hired for policing may be as high in developing countries in all regions as it is in Western Europe, North America, and Japan (2 per 1,000 population).[2] This contrasts sharply with the allocation of manpower to education or health services, which shows a progression along the continuum from "developing" to "developed" countries (from less than 2 to more than 20 per 1,000 population).

Fiscal resources: recurrent expenditures on crime control, insofar as reports are available, have averaged about 9 percent of

---

2. See pp. 103; 108, table 3; 116, table 7; 122, table 11; 126, table 15.

all governmental expenditures in Africa, 8 percent in Latin America, and 7 percent in Asia—with maxima much higher—compared with criminal justice outlays of about 3 percent in such developed countries as France, Japan, the United Kingdom, and the United States. It must be pointed out, of course, that the size of the country affects the percentage and that there could be some distortions if the percentages were not read in the light of the total figures involved.

Among those investment plans that include criminal policy, the median of capital allocation for crime control is about 2.5 percent, with maxima several times higher, owing usually to outlay on construction of correctional institutions and police accommodations. In this non-capital-intensive service, what is significant about this capital allocation is not only its own level but also the possible commitment that it implies to subsequent operating costs.

At the output end, one measure of what a criminal justice system does to people is the proportion of the population confined to correctional institutions on any one day.

There is the same surprising and unexplained range in developing as in developed countries, i.e., from 20 to more than 200 prisoners per 100,000 population. Although here there is no continuum along the "developing-to-developed" scale, there is some evidence of a negative relationship, in that the average for countries in the developing regions is as high as the maximum for Europe.

2. SOME TENTATIVE EXPLANATIONS

The reasons behind these at first sight surprising phenomena can only be guessed. A few tentative explanations may nevertheless be offered.

1. Problems of internal security are at least as great for the governments of developing as for those of developed countries, and in some cases may be greater.

2. Positive law is used as an instrument of social change

to at least as great an extent in developing as in developed countries.

3. Mobility and urbanization may be at least as disruptive of community value systems and controls in a developing country as in an industrially developed one.

4. A crucial development may be taking place, in which the state in a developing country may be substituting its justice for that of kinship groups.

5. Heavy outlay on crime control opens up certain kinds of tax-financed labor-intensive wage-paid or salaried employment in developing societies in which opportunities for paid employment are scarce.

6. A reciprocal relationship inevitably develops: expenditures on crime have an effect on the rates of crime which, in turn, will determine the level and kinds of need.

3. PLANNER'S DILEMMA

Faced with a social phenomenon such as crime which has not usually been thought of as having an obvious or consistent relationship to levels of economic development but which has undeniable financial implications and appears to vary inversely with the level of economic development, the planner naturally hesitates between two approaches.

On the one hand, he may think of criminal policy as something outside the field of economic development. The very concept of criminal justice implies human rights and the quality of life; and social development implies changes in the pattern of relationships between institutions as well as measurable increases in levels of consumption or length of life.

In view, however, of the relative magnitude of the resources allocated to crime control in developing countries, a planner may hesitate to dismiss them as "governmental overheads" or "expenses of sovereignty" immune from review. He may at least wish to regard them closely to make reasonably sure that they constitute a justifiable use of scarce resources when viewed in juxtaposition to other potentially competing uses, especially since the share of crime control in a nation's government-allocated resources is highest at the stage of development where these resources are least.

Nor is it only governmental resource allocation that is at issue. Planned development implies a high level of compliance with law, whereas lawbreaking adds to the uncertainties besetting a developer's calculations of the future, and some forms of crime add to the many factors destructive of productive resources, whereas the lessening of such risks contributes to the chances of economically productive investment.

In short, there would seem to be good reason why a government's development planners should be interested in getting value for the resources allotted to crime control and should, therefore, be interested in the cost-effectiveness of criminal policy even though this is seldom susceptible to exact calculation.

If the planning is sufficiently comprehensive to cover social as well as economic development, the planner may still find himself caught in a dilemma. Social planning implies governmental allocation of scarce resources to public social service programs. The development planner tends to give priority to those positive or constructive social service programs, such as education and health, that tend to expand with economic development. On the other hand, he is up against the fact that, in actual practice, crime control tends to be at or near the head of the list of priorities in governmental resource allocation among programs that critically affect social development. One trend in comprehensive planning has therefore been to approach criminal policy as a component of social development planning. Thus envisaged, criminal justice, like all public social services, is viewed as an authoritative expression of the extent and methods by which government uses its power for protecting human rights while also promoting economic and social change and development.

B. LEVELS OF PLANNING AGAINST CRIME

Planning for crime control or criminal justice occurs at three levels:

(1) Comprehensive economic and social development planning;
(2) Planning for the criminal policy sector as a single system;
(3) Planning for specific subsectors or subsystems in prevention of crime and treatment of offenders.

1. COMPREHENSIVE PLANNING

Analyzing the methods by which comprehensive development plans are prepared, it is apparent that they do not all approach comprehensive planning or criminal policy in the same way. Rather, it is possible to distinguish several typologies of comprehensive planning, each with its characteristic attitude toward crime control. Different typologies have been favored in different regions and, to a lesser extent, at different dates. (See C i below.)

Moreover, behind formal planning there is always a climate of opinion which again has not been constant but has evolved markedly over the quarter-century since the United Nations entered this field. (See C ii below.)

2. SECTORAL PLANNING

Planning for the criminal policy sector as a single coherent system implies a habit of thinking of it as a whole and defining a country's policy objective in terms of a model that is as broad as the system and embraces all its parts. This approach prevailed around 1800 but had been eclipsed by 1900 and is only now reemerging in the form of a contemporary criminal justice model. (See D i below.)

Because of the organized administrative unity of education

and health programs, sectoral planning of these services comes naturally and seems normal, both nationally and internationally. In criminal policy this is not yet so, and sectoral planning is still a trend rather than an achievement. (See D ii below.)

3. SUBSECTORAL PLANNING

Planning for specific subsectors or subsystems in the prevention of crime and treatment of offenders comes easier than planning for criminal policy as a whole, owing to the ill-coordinated diffusion of decision-making responsibility in most countries. For purposes of this study the following were considered and are discussed in more detail in section E below:

(a) Crime control in general:
    (i) Law enforcement planning (police);
    (ii) Judicial planning (penal law, prosecution, adjudication, sentencing);
    (iii) Correctional planning (treatment of offenders in institutions and in the community); and
(b) Juvenile delinquency control in particular:
    (iv) Juvenile delinquency planning.

C. COMPREHENSIVE PLANNING

1. TYPOLOGIES OF COMPREHENSIVE PLANNING IN RELATION TO CRIME

When one looks at national development plans to determine to what extent they take crime control into account, it becomes clear that they fall into several categories.

(a) At one extreme is what might be called the public administration or fiscal approach to planning. Its purpose is to facilitate budgeting for the next fiscal year by relating this to a four- or five-year capital investment plan. It therefore has to take account of the programs planned by every public service and then try to integrate them. Under these circumstances con-sideration is necessarily given to criminal policy and to all the governmental organs that plan and execute it. This approach is applicable at all governmental levels, and in internally self-governing territories as well as internationally sovereign countries. Economists working with this type of planning have tended to redefine social defense, i.e., the protection of society, as protection of developmental resources and processes, proclaiming that internal security is a prerequisite for the multiplication of productive resources. Inclusion of all aspects of criminal policy in development plans thus became the predominant approach on the part of comprehensive planners in most English-speaking countries in Africa, as well as in some other developing countries. Similarly, the national economic development plans of some developed countries with mixed economies began to explicitly include crime control among the services produced or consumed by government (Sweden, United Kingdom).

(b) At the other extreme is the kind of planning associated mainly with material production. Its purpose has been to facilitate the elaboration of economic policy so as to increase GNP. Because of these preoccupations it has either omitted crime control, as well as other governmental overheads, or has hesitatingly selected from it those few elements that it considers potentially productive.

(i) It became generally assumed among economic planners that the multiplication of productive resources, both physical and human, ought to have priority over allocation of resources to nonproductive purposes, including administration of criminal policy. Behind this was often the assumption that investments in health, housing, education, and labor would themselves make inroads on many social problems including crime, and that increased incomes would reduce the motivation for crime.

7

Therefore a development plan that made no reference to fighting crime might in the long run be the best way to prevent crime. Omission of direct reference to crime control thus became the predominant approach on the part of economics-oriented planners.

(ii) A less absolute approach was to accept the economic contention that scarce resources should be concentrated on multiplication of productive resources, but to include an educated and healthy population among these resources and to make small allocations to such aspects of social defense as might be described as rehabilitative of socially handicapped individuals, and therefore possibly productive. Token inclusion of social welfare aspects of social defense in development plans thus became characteristic of planning in India and some other countries.

(c) A completely different possibility has of course been to go beyond a fiscal or economic approach and to think of development as being many-sided or qualitative, and to regard the upbuilding of governmental and social institutions, including criminal justice, as being as valuable as the multiplication of productive resources. No development plans express this viewpoint explicitly; but it may be frequently implied. Even if formally omitted from an essentially economic development plan, the role of law and justice in economic and social development tends to be widely assumed.

2. CLIMATES OF OPINION REGARDING THE PLACE OF CRIME CONTROL IN DEVELOPMENT

The relationship between economic and social development and criminality was widely recognized by 1900, when the view became prevalent that a "positive" social policy concerned especially with improving education, health, employment, income, and housing opportunities could offer an alternative means of protecting society by giving priority to indirect prevention, rather than to direct deterrence, of crime. In this broad context, criminal policy and the specialized treatment of offenders remained important mainly as the last line of defense in the protection of society ("social defense," as it then came to be called on the European continent); it was "secondary and tertiary prevention."

This broad approach was implied in the assumption by the United Nations of leadership in promoting the study on an international basis of the problem of the prevention of crime and the treatment of offenders (1948), within the framework of which the more narrowly conceived functions of the International Penal and Penitentiary Commission were subsequently transferred to it.[3]

During the subsequent quarter century there have been wide changes in the climate of opinion, the net effect of which has been to shift attention from a simple, cause-and-effect relationship between development and crime toward consideration of a complex pattern of relationships that opened up new possibilities of planned intervention at many points. This change in approach may not be entirely unrelated to the change in membership of the United Nations as more developing countries joined and emphasized their needs.

(a) While governmental planning of resource allocation was being embarked upon as the key to economic development, it was also being recognized that neither increased output nor the development of positive social services could be counted on to prevent criminality. It became doubtful how far the positive causal relationship between an expanding supply of goods and services and a diminishing incidence of crime, which the

---

3. General Assembly resolution 415 (V) of December 1950.

criminologist of 1900 had hypothesized, might still hold good in developed countries in the mid-twentieth century.[4]

Some observers even went so far as to suggest a reverse causal relationship to the one that had previously been assumed: that, instead of being reduced by material affluence, criminality, like other forms of alienation or maladjustment, might have become part of the qualitative social price that was being paid for quantitatively measurable economic development.[5] At least one development plan explicitly justified its criminal policy outlay as one of the unavoidable costs of development (Uganda). This idea was sometimes applied to laissez-faire economic development, the inference being drawn that integrated national socioeconomic development planning might reduce these social costs of economic progress. It was also applied to the unexpected and deleterious side effects of dysfunctions of economic and social improvements, and to the ways in which programs were planned in detail, examples commonly cited being schooling unrelated to employment opportunities, or slum clearance and rehousing followed by increases in delinquency; from this there followed the contention that consultation with persons knowledgeable in crime might result in better planning at all levels and stages of the process. Thus envisaged, this "admission of criminologists to the planners' club" might result in

---

4. See *Report of the Fourth United Nations Congress on the Prevention of Crime and the Treatment of Offenders* (United Nations publication, Sales No. 71.IV.8).

5. See "Social Defence Policies in Relation to Development Planning," working paper prepared by the Secretariat for the Fourth United Nations Congress on the Prevention of Crime and the Treatment of Offenders (Kyoto, Japan, 17–26 August 1970) (A/CONF.43/1).

some diminution of the need or the demand for direct outlays on social defense.[6]

(b) The 1950s saw a differentiation between two complementary approaches to social policy. On the one side, a traditional distributive justice approach focused attention on the special needs of individuals in particularly disadvantaged minority categories, including offenders, and especially sentenced offenders, among others. This was the orientation thus favored by the developed nations which then represented a majority of member states. On the other side, a newer nation-building and community development approach gave general attention to the presumed universal needs of average people as members of families and neighborhoods. While the individual welfare approach had seemed natural in affluent and developed countries, the community-well-being approach seemed indispensable in poor and developing countries.

Insofar as social defense was interpreted as treatment of offenders as a category of socially handicapped persons, it now tended to be overlooked by this general movement toward broader measures on behalf of whole communities that were being bypassed by development. Hence, even in social policy planning the years around 1960 saw a temporary eclipse of concern with social defense viewed as a specialized service.

As it subsequently became clear, however, that concern with economic growth could not eliminate the need for social measures for lessening inequalities of opportunity, and that concern with general well-being could not eliminate the probability of disturbances of the social order, criminal policy came back in-

---

6. Fondation Internationale Pénale et Pénitentiaire et Société Internationale de Défense Sociale, *Criminalité et développement* (Milan, Centro Nazionale di Prevenzione e Difesa Sociale, 1970), volume prepared for the Fourth United Nations Congress on the Prevention of Crime and the Treatment of Offenders.

to focus as the protection of society's members, resources, and processes. It was to the criminal justice system in all its phases rather than to the offender's welfare that criminal policy now came to be again directed, and to its place as the protector of peaceful change and human rights in the complex pattern of a rapidly evolving society.

(c) During this generation the world of practice became permeated by the typically twentieth-century philosophical and scientific outlook that sought to understand life in terms of complex patterns of relationships between multitudes of different factors or variables and that believed it unrealistic to abstract simple sequences of cause and effect or means and ends from this complex whole, except perhaps under certain limited circumstances and for specific and defined purposes.

Lawbreaking came to be generally viewed, as Emile Durkheim had suggested long before, in relation to a cultural whole. Neither development and affluence nor underdevelopment and poverty could in themselves be now regarded as causes of crime.

Multiple changes in the culture might occur, however, giving new significance to various factors, and increasing certain probabilities of lawbreaking while lessening others. Migration between a rural and an urban milieu might thus weaken the social controls exercised traditionally by family and community, and at the same time put more weight on legal regulation of conduct, and therefore on the criminal justice system, in urban and rural areas alike. Even in a developed country, development might have aspects that favored certain tendencies more than others, as, for example, the multiplication of movable property susceptible to pilfering, the multiplication of mechanical vehicles endangering life and limb without criminal intent, the augmentation of physical facilities liable to vandalism, or the organization and protection of forbidden forms of free enterprise.

Attention was now given to such relationships between crime and society as the extent to which there was identification or alienation between the people and the law, the varying thresholds of public tolerance both of lawbreaking and of the criminal policy system, and the processes by which forms of nonconforming behavior are or are not labeled as offenses under criminal law.

Within the total evolving cultural pattern of a country, attention came to be focused on changes in the interrelations among its institutions, seen now as "interfaces" between component "systems," of which crime control could be envisaged as one among many. This favored new approaches to the organization of the treatment of offenders, such as the projection of education, health services, industrial management, social insurance, and safeguards for human rights, into the correctional process.

It was thus to some extent in ways such as these that new linkages were explored between crime in its many aspects and the culture to which it referred. The development in relation to which crime and its control had to be considered came now to be regarded in its total but diverse culture-changing pattern, with political and social change seen to be as relevant as economic growth.

The Second United Nations Congress on the Prevention of Crime and the Treatment of Offenders (London, 1960) considered reports on "types of criminality resulting from social changes and accompanying economic development," and the Third Congress (Stockholm, 1965) had on its agenda an item on "social change and criminality." On both occasions there was a call for deeper study of changes in criminality. On neither occasion was development regarded as being in itself criminogenic. Nevertheless, the Fourth United Nations Congress gave great prominence to the link, causal or otherwise, between crime and development. This indeed was the theme of the Congress held in Kyoto, Japan, in August 1970, and a declaration unanimously adopted by delegates from eighty countries stressed the inadequacies in the attention paid to all aspects of life in the process of development manifest in the increasing seriousness and proportions of the problem of crime in many countries and "the increasing urgency of the need for the world community of nations to improve its planning for economic and social development by taking greater account of the effects that urbanization, industrialization and the technological revolution may have upon the quality of life and the human environment." The congress called upon all governments "to take effective steps to co-ordinate and intensify their crime preventive efforts within the context of economic and social development which each country envisages for itself."

D. SECTORAL PLANNING

1. THE CONTEMPORARY CRIMINAL JUSTICE MODEL

Regardless of whether a country practices comprehensive development planning or includes criminal policy as part of such planning, it is possible for any government to think of criminal policy as a single sector.

This possibility is currently crystallizing into a trend toward a criminal justice model, widely acceptable in principle, although necessarily applicable in detail in different ways in different countries and regions.

Models play an important role as instruments of change, regardless of whether they are quantitative, as in economic development planning, or institutional, as in most social and political development.

Development planning and modernization tend to imply recognition of certain models as standards or goals toward which existing patterns of public policy should be oriented by means of a consciously planned strategy of change.

In criminal policy there have long been such models, which have spread widely from country to country. They have nevertheless changed remarkably in the industrially developed countries.

The eighteenth century completed the legitimization of the sovereign state using its monopoly of organized force to protect not only itself but also the persons and property of its citizens, and moving toward rational and utilitarian reforms of criminal codes and penal procedures conceived as complementary parts of a single whole.

In each developed sovereign state, the nineteenth century evolved not only some form or degree of threefold constitutional "separation of powers," under which responsibility for criminal policy was diffused among legislature, judiciary, and executive, but also a functional division of labor among separate state agencies concerned with specific subsectors of law and order, each of which tended to develop its own standards of professional ethics and technical competence, its own degree of budgetary initiative, and its own rate of growth: lawmaking, police, prosecution, adjudication, prisons, and eventually probation and parole, as well as juvenile delinquency control. This centrifugal model brought wide diffusion of responsibility and great difficulty in the way of thinking of criminal policy as a whole; but it fitted in with the tendency to downplay the role of criminal justice in preventing crime.

The twentieth century is witnessing the rise of a new criminal justice model which is already prevalent in the thinking of policymakers and informed observers, and which is gradually influencing policy decisions, organizational structures, operating procedures, and development planning. The outstanding characteristics of this contemporary developed model are:

(a) Thinking, studying, and planning in terms of a criminal justice system or sector as a whole, with special attention to critical points in an offender's path through and out of the system and to the interfaces between the specialized functional subsectors or subsystems, e.g., multiplication of laws or expansion of the police force as starting chain reactions throughout the system; safeguards of the rights of the offender that backfire by producing delays and injustice; pretrial in-

15

carceration as symptom and measure of overload in both the judicial and the penal subsystems; and the impact of judicial decisions on police action and prison occupancy. This implies integrated statistical reporting covering all subsectors of the criminal justice system, as an aid to unified planning.

(b) Recognition of the importance of information and communication as unifying common elements throughout the system, e.g., knowledge of the individual offender is useful to the procurator in making decisions concerning prosecution, to the judge in sentencing the convicted offender, and to the correctional administrator in formulating individual treatment programs. This implies coordinated record-keeping and transmittal in all crime control subsectors or subsystems, as an aid to operations.

(c) Opting for a criminal policy system aimed at criminal justice and not merely at crime control, protection of society, or internal security, with its recognition of an offender's rights, the quasi-judicial character of decisions taken at all stages of the offender's progress through and out of the system, and the consequent need to formalize all decisions respecting his rights, to assure due process and to safeguard against abuse or exceeding of authority.

(d) Recognition that sentencing does not deprive an offender of fundamental rights, that individualization can be sought through involving an offender in the programming of his correctional treatment, that work is a natural part of everyone's role in society rather than a servitude, and that institutional treatment ("deprivation of freedom") and community treatment ("treatment in freedom") are only two ends of a continuum of measures by which the sentenced offender is neither wholly deprived of fundamental freedoms nor allowed unguided enjoyment of them.

(e) Diversification of dispositional and correctional options, with reduction in reliance on maximum security institutions, special focus on degrees of freedom and of custody or supervision, including open institutions, halfway houses, weekend prisons, extramural work obligations, and conditional release, and administrative unification of all correctional options in a single agency.

(f) Decriminalization in locally acceptable selected aspects of law and procedure as a means of reducing the overload on the criminal justice system, e.g., abolition of penalties on victimless consensual behavior (public drunkenness, vagrancy, prostitution, adult homosexuality, gambling, abortion, etc.); abolition of penalties for acts committed by juveniles which would not be criminal if committed by adults; downgrading of offenses from felonies to misdemeanors to violations; increased decision of cases at the police or procuratorial phase rather than by formal trial and conviction; simplification of fiscal and other administrative regulations so as to diminish the risk of violation; substitution of administrative for judicial tribunals ("no fault" work injuries and traffic accidents); substitution of administrative for quasi-judicial or judicial sanctions for dangerous behavior without criminal intent (suspension of licenses); substitution of "civil" for "penal" treatment (drug and alcohol addiction); etc. In every region, some of these forms of decriminalization are more favored than others.

(g) Adaptation of policies and programs for defining and preventing crime and treating offenders in a mobile and urbanizing culture that embraces conflicting value systems, including the offender's involvement in the achievement of shared goals through locally legitimized forms of community participation in his treatment, and the rethinking in dynamic terms of the offender's personality growth, motivation, maturation, and self-image.

(h) Increasing crime prevention by environmental management (street lighting; car-door locking; building design; control of trade in arms, drugs, etc.; substitution of checking for cash; mass media; etc.)

(i) Reorientation of criminological research from social and

17

individual cause assignment and prediction into a policy science concerned with systems analysis, cross-sectoral policy planning, cost-effectiveness measurement, behavioral study of planned change, etc.

2. TRENDS TOWARD SECTORAL PLANNING AGAINST CRIME

Countries that have set up machinery looking toward integrated planning in the criminal justice sector include:

Chile—Social Defense Planning Section in the Ministry of Justice and National Criminal Justice Coordinating Council;

Kenya—Prime Minister's Office directly responsible for all Internal Security;

Philippines—Peace and Order Council, Committee on Crime Prevention and Treatment;

Somali Democratic Republic—Advisory Committee on Criminal Policy;

United Kingdom—Coordinating Council on the Penal System;

Venezuela—Crime Prevention Section in the Ministry of Justice.

In one federal country, the national government recently began to make grants-in-aid to its component states for state and local law enforcement, conditional on each state setting up a comprehensive crime control planning agency and submitting each year a revised comprehensive plan, although these are only gradually moving from collection of unconnected projects toward integrated state criminal justice planning (United States).

Recognizing the crucial importance of this question, the United Nations has sought to promote more integrated criminal justice planning as part of comprehensive national development planning. At several recent United Nations meetings and in a number of publications the need for this kind of approach, the problems involved and the ways and means of translating it into practice have been considered.[7] Some of the aspects have been referred to in this survey before; they cannot be dealt with in detail here, but the significance of such an integrated approach both for more wholesome national development and for more consistent and effective criminal justice administration needs to be reiterated. There appears to be some evidence that the need for it is becoming more widely appreciated, but much remains to be done. Progress in this respect will require continuous sensitization of planners to the interrelationships involved, particularly the link between dysfunctional, inadequately planned development and crime, and the acquaintance of those working in the field of crime with the methods and techniques of planning. The continuous refinement of these methods and the introduction of new ones will be an essential task of those seeking to devise more effective development strategies in the different countries in the years to come.

E. SUBSECTORAL PLANNING

The criminal justice system is here examined in terms of four major subsystems on the work loads of which all governments may be presumed to keep administrative records, and for which

---

7. See e.g. *Report of the Fourth United Nations Congress on the Prevention of Crime and the Treatment of Offenders,* Kyoto, Japan, 17-26 August 1970 (United Nations publication, Sales No. 71.IV.8), pp. 7-13; Report of the *Ad Hoc* Meeting of Experts on "Social Defence Policies in Relation to Development Planning," Rome, 24-30 June 1969 (E/CN.5/C.3/R.4/Rev.1), and *A Policy Approach to Planning in Social Defence* (United Nations publication, Sales No. 72.IV.9).

they necessarily budget outlays both on current operations and on capital facilities. These include:

(i)   Law enforcement
(ii) Judicial process
(iii) Correctional treatment
(iv) Juvenile delinquency services

These are established and well-recognized entities, each of which tends to plan separately for its own separate development. This has often led to fragmentation and bottlenecks stemming from policies which are inconsistent and sometimes operating at cross-purposes. It has not adequately furthered the development and operational efficiency of the criminal justice system (or rather, "nonsystem") as a whole, which requires a more comprehensive and integrated approach recognizing the basic interrelationships of the component parts. Attempts at more integrated criminal justice planning made recently in some countries have been spurred by the realization of the essential inadequacy of a purely segmental approach and the problems which it has tended to perpetuate and even create (e.g., prison overcrowding exacerbated by stricter or more efficient law enforcement coupled with excessive delays in the administration of justice). A consistent criminal policy would have to conceive of criminal justice as an organic whole whose elements interact and are, in turn, affected by this very interaction. The question of how to put this approach into effect operationally and how to integrate it with broader national planning remains a major task confronting planners and those working in the criminal justice field alike.

1. LAW ENFORCEMENT

Effective crime control presupposes a law-abiding people, that is to say, a population that identifies to a high degree with authority and law, as well as police action to increase the probability of the population complying with the law. Different development plans, therefore, indicate widely different degrees of reliance on public cooperation and on policing. One possibility is the state in which public cooperation with guardians of the peace can be taken for granted and is organized. A different possibility is the state in which significant elements in the population do not share in the behavior patterns or developmental processes sanctioned by law, and in which the threshold of acceptance of authority may be low and reliance on police action may be high in relations between the government and some segments of the population. A third possibility is the state that leaves large areas of behavior for unofficial regulation in accordance as much with custom as with law, as in the kinship groups of Africa, the village communities of Southern Asia, or the plantation societies of tropical America.

The threshold of compliance may vary greatly in respect of different kinds of prohibited behavior. At one extreme, a population may cooperate in the protection of life and property and the regulation of those aspects of everyday living that directly affect their own immediate well-being while not recognizing the legitimacy of the government, as in a militarily occupied country or territory. At the other extreme, a population may be loyal to its form of government but tolerant of breaches of certain of its laws. This latter situation may often arise through attempts "to write morality into law." There are, for example, development plans in which it has been proposed to ban commercial prostitution or the trade in alcohol, without its being possible for the police to enforce the law in a uniform and therefore equitable manner, thus increasing the probability of police partiality and corruption and popular disrespect for law, to be followed by eventual silent abandonment of these objectives of the plan.

The modern state is usually conceived of as a group whose government, in order to serve its people, has achieved a monopoly of force within its territory. There are, however, various degrees of approximation to this classical model. There are, for example, countries in which patrons uphold clients by retaining armed guards, landlords and tenants or management and labor settle their differences by violence, armed robber bands live off the land, secret societies extort protection money, criminal tribes live by despoiling others, "organized crime" enforces its own rules, armed political organizations have been permitted to arise, or groups of local people are allowed to take law into their own hands through vigilantism. Some development plans reflect a strengthening of police forces for the purpose of counteracting this diffusion of force and consolidating the sovereignty of government.

The functions of a police force vary greatly from country to country. In some, there may be a number of specialized police forces, as for example for preventive patrol, criminal investigation, border control, traffic control, enforcement of health or building regulations, pursuit of tax delinquency, or protection of the authorities, whereas in others there may be one all-inclusive police force or a single safety and protection force responsible also for fire fighting and handling all emergencies. Again, a police force may be limited to prevention and investigation of crime; or its functions may extend into the prosecution of offenses; it may even be entrusted with certain adjudicatory or dispositional power, especially with regard to juvenile offenders, as in some countries of Eastern Asia; or it may have custody of prisoners, protection of the prison perimeter, or supervision of ex-prisoners.

There are thus many differences that have to be taken into account when reviewing the place of policing in criminal policy and in governmental development plans.

Some aspects of police development admit of external financing; these include communication and transportation equipment; and this is perhaps one reason why there has been a widespread tendency to include capital outlay on police in development plans. Another large item has been the construction of police stations, police repair shops, police training centers and staff colleges, and above all police housing—this last representing perhaps a preference for a once-for-all development outlay on remuneration in kind rather than a recurring operational expenditure on higher wages.

Police everywhere represent the biggest item in the direct crime control work force. In Sweden the plan target for 1970 was 220 per 100,000 population in the police, plus another 100 in courts and penal care; in the United Kingdom, authorized police strength has increased to 220 per 100,000 population; in the United States police are at nearly the same ratio, while the total personnel engaged in criminal justice there has reached 360 per 100,000. Many developing countries are approaching these ratios in spite of being less urbanized.

2. THE JUDICIAL PROCESS

Insofar as the development of criminal justice implies the development of written law and of a legal profession that interprets and applies it, several questions pose themselves urgently to development planners.

One is how to keep the standards of behavior sanctioned by the law as close as possible to those acceptable to the bulk of the population. A peculiar difficulty presents itself where there is a clash between two legal systems, as for example an adopted system of positive law and an endogenous system or set of systems of customary law. Several development plans, especially in Africa, make provision for research looking toward the eventual unification of these systems; they seem to be approaching this as much by way of early codification as by the kind of appellate recourse and case recording that would gradually evolve a common law.

Another problem is how to define the relationship between professional and lay justice. In Africa, priority is given to the extension of magistrates' tribunals as a substitute for the former judicial role of the civil administrator. In Asia, on the other

23

hand, priority is given in development plans to the revival or creation of popular tribunals, to provide an inexpensive alternative to professional law courts and a means of lessening the likelihood of minor disputes flaring into crimes. In both regions it is government policy to have popular tribunals coexist with professional law courts. The tendency seems to be to have the two kinds of courts serve as alternatives rather than as substitutes for one another, and to make the decisions of popular tribunals binding only insofar as they have the consent of the parties and are in accordance with the law.

An almost universal problem concerns investment in the physical facilities required for professional justice. Capital outlay included in development plans has been mainly for court-houses, judges' and magistrates' living quarters, law schools, and centers for training court officers.

Plans seldom if ever provide for the continuing study and reform of the actual operation of criminal law and procedures. Some nevertheless take account of judicial powers and practices as these affect investment in a physical plant.

A few development plans reflect concern over the degree of sentencing discretion vested in courts of law. On the one hand, they may welcome a tendency to widen the range of options at the disposal of judges, as by so altering the law as to authorize open prisons, supervised probation, compensation of the victim, and other rehabilitation- or restitution-oriented penalties. On the other hand, they may have to accept a policy trend, evident in Africa, to limit judicial discretion by placing on the courts a statutory obligation to impose mandatory or minimum deterrence-oriented sentences, or by reserving to the government recourse on appeal against what it considers too light a sentence. Either way, the powers given to the courts and the way they exercise them have a marked impact on the amount and kind of correctional accommodation for which provision has to be made in state investment planning.

One recent Latin American development plan proposes to

reduce the need for institutions by reducing the number of persons awaiting trial who are confined there. The proportion of persons awaiting trial is reported to be very high: one third or more in some countries of Western Europe and North America; one half around the eastern Mediterranean; and, in countries of Latin America, from 50 to 75 percent.[8] . . . In some countries it has nevertheless proved possible to speed up trials without doing injustice to the persons charged and by leaving most persons at liberty during the short time while they are awaiting trial. Some problems of facilities needed in the correctional subsector have thus been demonstrated to be susceptible to solution by modification of services rendered in the subsector of prosecution and adjudication; of this, however, the development plans offer only infrequent evidence.

Plans refer even less to the problem of civil imprisonment for not obeying court orders to pay fines, to support a family, or to meet other debts. This practice may account for a significant proportion of the prison population in some countries, calling attention to important issues concerning the place of fines in a criminal justice system and the role of court action in a total scheme for providing for mothers and children, and may therefore indicate an area susceptible of handling in a planning context.

3. CORRECTIONAL TREATMENT
Those development plans which include correction care tend to adopt one of two approaches.

Most approach this as a matter of capital outlay on the construction of institutions. Insofar as they consider alternatives, it is mainly in order to keep down the cost of institutions and to increase their contribution to production, as for example by

---

8. *International Review of Criminal Policy*, No. 26 (1968), pp. 19, 79 (United Nations publication, Sales No.:70.IV.1).

promoting prison industries or, to an even greater extent, prison farms. With this is sometimes linked some planning for comparatively low-cost "open" institutions, especially in rural Africa; and one plan proposes to change its code of penal procedure so as to legalize open prisons. On the whole there seems to be a preference for small- or medium-sized institutions, for reasons of geographical dispersal and easy transportation; but occasionally a country with considerable resources will plan a mammoth institution or complex of institutions. Some plans include special institutions for young offenders, sometimes under such borrowed names as borstals, detention centers, and reformatories.[9]

An alternative planning approach has been to put the emphasis on the human resources confined in institutions and the possibility of reintegrating them into the productive activities of the community in other ways besides relating institutional labor to work done outside. No known plan takes this developmental viewpoint consistently and systematically; but some include token provision for prison social work and aftercare. The same plans often also include token provision of specialized institutions for the correction of beggars, vagrants, and prostitutes and, in a few cases, drug addicts. This approach is usually associated with social welfare and occasionally with health services.

No known comprehensive development plan deals with corrections as a whole or considers systematically the possible substitution of services for buildings—of limitation of freedom ("treatment in the community") in place of suspension or deprivation of freedom ("institutional treatment")—although some propose to reduce overcrowding by paroling prisoners or suspending sentences. There are nevertheless some countries that

---

9. *The Young Adult Offender* (United Nations publication, Sales No. 65.IV.5).

have reduced prison overcrowding and avoided prison construction by a policy of developing alternatives to imprisonment (e.g., Japan). Heavier reliance on extramural services than on institutional facilities may be more characteristic of "post-industrial" service economies than of most developing countries.

In spite of the focusing of development plans on institutional facilities requiring considerable capital investment rather than on services requiring mainly recurrent expenditure, no plan has appeared in which provision is made for systematically implementing the United Nations Standard Minimum Rules for Treatment of Prisoners, even in countries which have formally incorporated them into their criminal legislation or prison regulations. This is serious from a developmental viewpoint, since there are countries with development plans in which rehabilitation, in the sense of the preparation of offenders for a return to lawful self-support in freedom, may be impeded by custodial routine and incomplete application of provisions designed to safeguard basic human rights in penal establishments. The nearest any country has come to including Standard Minimum Rules implementation in its development plan has been India, which at the end of its second plan period established a Central Bureau of Correctional Services, in harmony with the advice of a United Nations technical assistance mission, the powers of which, however, have remained purely advisory owing to the omission from subsequent plans of federal grants-in-aid of state correctional planning.

Failure to plan alternative ways of disposing of sentenced persons seems to be associated with high use of penal institutions in some developing countries.

To get a rough notion of the order of magnitude of the work load of correctional institutions, one may look at the ratio of prisoners to population, remembering that there are seasonal fluctuations as well as variations from one series of years to another. In developed countries of recent years, and in round figures, the number of nonjuvenile prisoners per 100,000 population has ranged from 20 in the Netherlands or 50 in France or Japan to 100 in Canada and 200 in the United States. The range in the developing countries is equally great in Asia and Latin America, and is still greater in Africa where four countries report ratios in excess of that of the United States, with South Africa peaking at 400. It would appear that, as a general rule and in spite of some exceptions, a lower proportion of the population is in prison in Europe and Japan than in most other regions of the world.

In addition to deprivation of freedom by detention in regular prisons, some countries make special arrangements under some circumstances for confinement of persons deemed politically dangerous. Such arrangements seem to be uniformly additional to such general provisions as may be made under correctional development planning. Forced labor by political prisoners for general development purposes is limited under General Assembly resolution 758 (VIII) of 1953, administered by the International Labor Organisation.

4. JUVENILE DELINQUENCY SERVICES

Many development plans recognize an increase in the extent to which the upbringing of children and adolescents is no longer regarded as simply a family problem but as a social problem, requiring special services promoted or provided by government.

Many governments provide—and some of these make provision in their plans—for what they regard as preventive social welfare services on behalf of those of their younger citizens who seem to be in need of more care and protection than their families provide. Insofar as these services are of a primarily preventive nature, they are not considered here, although some plans do include provision for constructing congregate facilities for housing and rearing homeless and neglected children, for housing young persons who have left their families to come to urban areas in search of work or training, and for accommodating family tribunals.

Other such child welfare services may be more directly related to lawbreaking; thus, some plans include construction of probation offices and hostels so as to facilitate "treatment in freedom," as well as capital outlay on children's reception centers, corrective schools, and juvenile tribunals. These are usually to help children who need care and protection or control as well as those who have broken the law. Plans more frequently include services as well as facilities in the case of juvenile delinquents than in that of adult offenders.

Some plans which do not include crime control in general nevertheless include services for preventing juvenile delinquents and predelinquents from growing into adult lawbreakers, regarding this limited form of "social defense" as being as constructive and productive as investment in education or health. Such provision, however, is frequently planned at a token level.

As social programs specializing in education, health, and social welfare develop, their interface with the old established criminal policy system might be expected to become important. In fact, in the development plans of developing countries the criminal justice subsector in which the first significant intersectoral impact occurs is the newest subsector, juvenile delinquency control; and the first of the newer social programs to have impact on it is neither education nor health but social welfare.

As in other criminal policy subsectors, not all important recent developments are reflected in development plans, especially if they turn on services and procedures not directly related to investment in facilities.

Thus, no available plan gives evidence of the innovative ways in which some countries of Eastern Asia are adapting traditional attitudes toward child status to modern circumstances and institutions, and particularly to the role of the police and their volunteer collaborators in supplementing the role of the family.

29

2

REGIONAL ANALYSES

A. AFRICA

1. COMPREHENSIVE PLANNING IN RELATION TO CRIME

Governments of African countries provide more evidence than those of any other developing region concerning the relationship between criminal policy and comprehensive development planning. This is because the dominant plan model, especially in all English-speaking countries of this region, tends to differ from that prevailing in other regions, in that it covers all governmental activities so as to provide a basis for annual budgeting and external aid. On questions of crime control planning, development plans therefore provide as much data from Africa alone as from all other developing regions together. This also permits somewhat deeper analysis, in each subsector, of the problems faced, their dimensions and complicating factors, and the classical and innovative solutions that are being attempted.

Inclusion of Criminal Policy in Comprehensive Planning

General development plans in African countries illustrate the widest possible range of attitudes toward the relationship between criminal policy and development planning.

At one extreme is the model more dominant here than elsewhere—the many plans that include an important crime control sector which they justify explicitly or implicitly in terms of the relevance of crime control to development. Kenya, for example, has consistently prefaced the internal security chapter of its plans with a statement of the direct bearing of law and order on economic and social development, declaring in a recent plan: "Without internal security, it is not possible to maintain an atmosphere conducive to rapid development. Experience has shown that failure to maintain internal security can lead to loss of confidence, economic stagnation or even recession."[10] The transitional development plan for Zambia (1965–66) gave to "the classical functions of government" including "internal security" a priority equal to that given to manpower development. A Uganda plan (1966–71) recognized an increase in crime but believed it might be a normal aspect of an increase in economic activity. Countries in this group have planned to devote between 1 and 10 percent of their public investment to crime control.

Near to this full-inclusion extreme are those plans which include crime control, but only for the purpose of reducing it, like all other governmental expenditures, to the lowest possible minimum, in order to concentrate on directly productive investments. These include plans of Benin and Senegal and the capital budget of Algeria, which allow less than 1 percent for investment in crime control.

One plan omits capital outlay on courts and prisons but includes that on police, gendarmerie, and juveniles (Central African Republic).

Several plans have omitted police and justice as governmental overheads but have included prevention and treatment of juvenile delinquency as part of a social development sector (Chad, Ethiopia, Somali Democratic Republic, and Tunisia).

Nonmention of Criminal Policy
in the Comprehensive Plan

---

10. Kenya, *Development Plan for the Period 1970 to 1974* (Nairobi, 1969), p. 548.

At the other extreme are those development plans which completely omit provisions for internal as well as external security. These include the plans of Algeria, Burundi, Cameroon, Congo (Brazzaville), Gabon, Libya, Madagascar, Niger, Senegal, and South Africa, as well as Equatorial Guinea (1964–67). These have been joined by the recent or current plans for Ethiopia (1968–73), Somalia (1971–77), and Sudan (1970–75), the last of which says of the plan for the previous decade: "In its essence the Plan did not formulate major trends and patterns of economic and social development; rather it was mere compilation of numerous unco-ordinated projects . . ."; but the new plan may implicitly include social defense among the capital investments for "central administration," for which there is no detailed breakdown. Exclusion of criminal policy from an investment plan does not imply low resource allocation to this purpose.

Reasons for the Place of Crime Control Facilities in Investment Planning in Africa

The exceptional importance attached to capital outlay for crime control in African planning may be attributable partly to the cost of setting up new independent states and endowing them with the basic physical facilities and services believed necessary for their national unity and internal security, especially since many were formed from the breakup of federal territorial groupings. Recognition of the importance of internal security for development does not necessarily imply future continuance of capital investment on crime control at the same high level. It is possible, for example, that heavy outlay on setting up a unified system of law courts, police quarters, and prisons may be a phase associated with independence and nation-building, so that emphasis on plan outlays for capital investment may be followed by concern with budget outlays on recurrent expenditures. It is also possible that in this later phase criminal policy might contribute more to development by developing less expensive means of treating offenders, of which examples will be given later, as well as more community participation in policing and justice, of which the plans do not yet give any evidence. There is, however, no evidence of any clear trend: among countries from which both current and earlier plans are available, approximately one half indicate increases and one half decreases in the share of crime control in development investment. There is no ground for saying that criminal policy expenditures now receive lower priority than was the case in the colonial period, especially in view of continuing or growing concern with internal security.

One incentive to the preparation of comprehensive development plans has been the need to satisfy the requirements of bilateral and multilateral aid programs. The criminal policy items in these plans may subsequently have turned out to be to some extent unsuitable for external financing. Actual investment may therefore have fallen short of planned investment. Uganda reports, for example, that target investment on law and order was 12 percent of the total in the public sector, whereas actual outlay turned out to be only 3 percent under its second plan (1966–71).

Recurrent Expenses

Some African plans take account of recurrent expenditures with a view to indicating how much these would be increased by increasing investments in a sector. The targets set indicate that the share envisaged for crime control in an African government's total recurrent expenditures may frequently be expected to approximate one tenth and may even reach one fifth. Annual operating budgets confirm this estimate. This is the region in which the highest proportion of budgeted expenditures goes for crime control. In one country, 9,000 of 36,000 government personnel are in police, gendarmerie, prisons, and law courts (Malagasy Republic). In some, more is spent on police and prisons than on education. During the ten years 1963/1973, the share of criminal policy in operating expenses has risen in Botswana, Ethiopia, Kenya, and Mauritius while declining in

Malta, South Africa, and Zambia. Where budget appropriations for other functions are increasing rapidly, the relative share of crime control may show some sign of slipping.

2. EXTENT OF INTEGRATED PLANNING IN THE CRIMINAL POLICY SECTOR

Most African countries plan crime control investments in terms of specific projects under three or four different ministries: usually interior or home affairs for police and sometimes prisons; justice for courts and sometimes prisons; social affairs or community development for juvenile delinquency; and, in French-speaking countries, defense or armed services for gendarmerie. On the other hand, a few, such as Kenya, have planned all these subsectors as part of a single internal security sector related directly to the head of government. It is also reported that the Somali Democratic Republic has established an advisory committee on criminal policy, composed of the president of the supreme court, the attorney general, and the commandants of the police and the customs.

Problems of sector definition are as difficult in Africa as everywhere. For reasons of practical convenience, this survey is confined to easily identifiable costs related directly to the control of crime and the treatment of offenders. On the other hand, it excludes such other specialized activities as city planning, education, and employment opportunities, important though these indirect but "positive" contributions may or may not be to prevention of crime.

A particular instance of this exclusion is provided by several African countries which have national youth services which presumably lessen the risk of lawbreaking by unemployed young persons. Investment in these services is indirectly rather than directly related to crime control. It is therefore regarded as a sector separate from crime control, in all national plans as well as in this survey. Nevertheless, Tanzania planned to use its national service as a recruiting ground for both police and army.

Armies are also distinguished from crime control in this

report. The boundary is nevertheless unclear, as when Tanzania allocates policing duties to its military air wing, or the Uganda Rifles help put down armed cattle-raiding, or the Botswana police serve as border guards in the absence of an army, or mobile armed police (gendarmerie) come under a ministry of defense as in francophone countries.

Border patrol is another area in which allocation of responsibilities is not uniform. While some countries, like Tanzania, have planned for a special immigration service, others have relied on police or gendarmerie, and Ghana planned armed border settlements and separated its border patrol from its police in the mid-1960s, before later reintegrating these two forces.

3. SUBSECTORAL PLANNING

The emergence of newly independent states in Africa has been accompanied by a considerable building up of governmental overheads, including police, law courts, prisons, and juvenile services, each of which poses some special planning problems.

a. Law Enforcement

Dimensions of the problem. The regular state police forces are gradually reaching out into all population centers and are beginning to penetrate into the villages, besides reaching their highest density in capital cities, at ports of entry, along lines of rail, and in areas being opened up for mineral exploitation. The most policed countries of Africa are now approaching as high a proportion of police to total population as is usual in the most developed countries of the North Atlantic region, i.e., 2 per 1,000, and many other African countries have as high a police-to-population ratio as the rural parts of developed countries, namely 1 per 1,000. In sparsely populated countries, it may nevertheless be difficult to have enough police to cover the whole territory; the Botswana plan thus contrasts its one policeman per 500 square kilometers with the 1 per 100 of Zambia and the 1 per 35 of Malawi.

One country has explicitly set 2 police per 1,000 population as its goal, even to the point of estimating that a 3.5 percent annual growth in population will require a 7 percent annual rise in police outlay (Swaziland, 1973–77). Another plans to reach 1.7 per 1,000 by 1981, at a cost of an additional 9 percent per year in recurrent expenditure (Uganda, 1971–76).

Complicating factors. In addition to the regular state police, many African countries have had other policing systems, such as the messengers of civil administrators, the agents through whom customary chiefs have maintained order, and in Nigeria the Native Authority Police. An important current trend is therefore toward a unified police establishment. A Ghanaian plan, for example, has declared: "The opportunity will be taken during this period to reduce the number of escort police and to increase the general police branch, the ultimate aim being, as literacy spreads, to abolish the escort branch and replace them by general police, all of whom will be literate. The opportunity will also be taken to gradually absorb the local authority police forces and to abolish such forces as they are taken over."[11] The Ghanaian state police establishment was doubled during that period by the inclusion of the former Native Authority Escort Police.

The spread of literacy plays an important part in the development of African police forces, opening up the privilege of regular pay and a career opportunity for some of the young men who have attended primary school, and marking the differences between the newer state police and the older nonliterate native authority escorts.

Nor is Ghana alone to comment on rising standards among the police; the Uganda plan states: "Standards of living are rising rapidly in Uganda amongst those sections of the com-

---

11. Ghana, *Second Development Plan, 1959–1964* (Accra, 1959).

munity from which the police are drawn. The educational standard for entry to the police has also been rising over the last few years. In consequence, it is necessary for the maintenance of morale to provide improved living conditions for members of the forces."[12]

The breakup of previous colonial groupings of territories has increased the length of boundaries to be patrolled. A million refugees have moved across the borders; armed infiltration is not unknown; differential administered prices have encouraged contraband; customs duties have had to be administered; and immigrants have had to be registered. Border patrolling by both land and water is mentioned by several countries as a reason for expanding their police forces (Botswana, Ghana, Kenya, Lesotho, Tanzania, and Uganda, among others).

Migratory pastoral populations pose a special problem. One particular form that it takes is stock theft, the prevention of which is among the reasons given for police expansion in several countries, including Tanzania which has created special units for this purpose. In some instances, including Kenya and Uganda, this interlocks with the boundary problem. In Somalia, the police have assisted in land settlement and community development around their police posts.

Solutions envisaged. Most African countries have planned an expansion of their police forces and the construction of new police posts: Botswana, a 45 percent increase in personnel in the first two years of internal self-government (1965–67) and the building of six new police stations, one in an area where important developments were occurring and another in a remote border area (1966–71); the Central African Republic, 170 additional police besides gendarmes (1966–70); Ivory Coast, a doubling of its gendarmerie, besides establishing more police

---

12. Uganda, *The First Five-Year Development Plan, 1961/1962 to 1965/1966* (Kampala, 1961).

posts on the borders (1960-70); Kenya, eight new police posts in the first three years of independence; Tanzania, a 20 percent increase in its police force and over 40 new police stations (1964-69); and Uganda, a doubling of the central government police during the 1960s, to be followed by another doubling in the 1970s, along with a hope that there will be a police station in each subdivision of a county by the year 2000.

The greatest object of capital outlay on police in Africa is their housing. This accommodation amounts to about half of total police investment, and since independence there has been much catching up on arrears. The provision of police "lines" seems to be universal. One current plan, which describes its police as "undermanned and underhoused," aims at building almost as many housing units as there are policemen (Uganda, 1971-76). In addition to its being expected as a fringe benefit, several plans justify it on the ground that the policeman is not free to choose his own place of residence, that it should be possible to deploy a police force rapidly, and that security reasons also tell in favor of publicly provided housing. Some say that this will save the government the cost of paying housing allowances, i.e., capital investment is substituted for recurrent expenditures. Two have suggested that, in the long run, government should plan to recover the construction cost by charging rent (Lesotho), or should have local communities build houses to rent to the police (Morocco); and one opines that subsidized housing for police and other public officials may have deterred private investment in housing, with resulting shortages, high rents, demands for increased housing allowances, and therefore pressure for more subsidized house-building (Uganda, 1971). With police quarters may come also some police welfare facilities, such as recreation halls and, in Uganda, a boarding school for their children. The social cost of this widespread policy may be some degree of separation between police and public.

All African countries including police in their plans have at-

39

tempted to improve the quality of police work. Thus all have planned also for police training centers, combined, however, in one case with the training of immigration officials (Tanzania) and in another with the school of public administration (Niger). Occasionally separate provision has been made for a senior police college (Ghana, Nigeria) or a gendarmerie school (Ivory Coast). An increase in educational level has been aimed at (Ghana, Uganda), as well as increased capability to investigate sophisticated offenses. Most of all, there has been an increase in specialization as between uniformed patrol, criminal investigation, and surveillance (Central African Republic, Uganda).

As part of this improvement in the quality of police work, nearly all African countries have planned to increase their degree of motorization, including development of repair shops and mobile units. Some have developed radio networks. A few have developed laboratories (Central African Republic, Mauritius). Less frequently they plan to improve police stables (Lesotho for horses, Sudan for camels).

b. Law and Law Courts

Several governments have planned the modernization of their law, although this is a long process unlikely to be completed in one plan period.[13] It has several aspects. One is the creation of a common law which will be the same for all inhabitants regardless of their origin. Another is the "restatement" in writing of those parts of the customary law that give rise to most disputes, because "today few tribesmen are familiar with customary law, as new patterns of work prevent their regular attendance at tribal gatherings and parts of the law itself are confused as the

---

13. For African traditions of restitution and group responsibility, see *Revue internationale de droit pénal*, Vol. 39, No. 1–2 (Paris, 1968).

result of attempts to accommodate it to more rapidly changing situations.''[14] Another again is the fusion into a single code of positive and customary law. One country plans the adoption of Swahili as the language of the courts (Tanzania). One has planned a law development center to combine the training of magistrates and lawyers with law reporting, law reform and revision, legal and criminological research, and the archiving of legal materials (Uganda).

Nigeria plans to build new courthouses as part of the administrative infrastructure of the states into which it has now been subdivided (1970).

Several countries are extending their salaried magistracy down into the rural communities in supplementation or substitution of the customary authorities (Guinea, additional *juges de paix*; Ivory Coast, 53 *juges de paix*; Morocco, planned outlay on primary tribunals in early 1960s; Uganda, 190 magistrates' houses; Zambia, 25 local court buildings). This may be symbolized by new rural courthouses. Kenya, after replacing its "African courts" with "district magistrates' courts," commented: "Many of the former African court buildings were temporary structures built of mud and wattle or sundried bricks, while, in some cases, cases were heard under a tree due to lack of court buildings.''[15] Tanzania has planned for local communities to meet half the cost of new rural courthouses. Uganda has justified the planning of housing for second- and third-grade magistrates, in that "lack of magistrates' housing makes it extremely difficult to develop the integrated judiciary as a unified service, free from local pressures." It has also commented on the interaction between increased courts and increased need for

---

14. Botswana, *National Development Plan, 1970–75* (Gaberone, 1970).

15. Kenya, *Development Plan for the Period 1970 to 1974* (Nairobi, 1970).

police: "Another factor that is making extra demands on the police force is the integration of local courts with the central government court system. The police are directly involved in prosecution work in courts and in the giving of evidence, and this increase in work places a great burden on them even if procedures can be introduced to reduce court delays."[16]

Most countries are introducing a separation of function between area civil administrator and local magistrate and are providing the magistrates with their own courts and housing. In one country, the planned capital outlay for this purpose is as high as for police (Lesotho). In another, four fifths of the investment in justice is in houses for judges (Swaziland).

The new developments have sometimes required planning for the training of court clerks to ensure record-keeping (Botswana, Uganda), or for the training of local-level magistrates (Zambia).

One country plan notes that a "customary courts commissioner" has relieved the area civil administrators of their former supervision of customary courts, and that these can be empowered to administer any written law, thus "paving the way for the future primary court and a single judicial system."[17]

Behind the plans one notes a trend in Africa toward criminalization rather than decriminalization; and this is probably a major factor in the expansion of police and corrections as well as law courts. The policy of substituting governmental for customary justice, with accompanying changes in substantive law, is one aspect of this. Thus, in many countries it has now become a crime for a kinship group to do justice on behalf of a member, as with the revolutionary Somali criminalization of the vendetta. There has also been a

16. Uganda, *Work for Progress: Uganda's Second Development Plan, 1966-1971* (Kampala, 1966).

17. Botswana, *National Development Plan, 1970-75* (Gaberone, 1970).

multiplication of governmental regulations of people's behavior, with the result that many fall foul of the law by violating regulations, including those dealing with identity cards, immigration formalities, unlicensed business activities, and trespassing on land that is now regarded as governmental or private property.

c. Treatment of Offenders[18]

Dimensions of the problem. African countries rely heavily on custodial treatment of prisoners. Although some make little use of prisons, others make far more use of them than is usual in Europe or Asia, and a few equal or surpass the Americas in ratio or prisoners to population. The increase in the number of prisoners seems to have run ahead of the increase in accommodation in most countries, so that severe overcrowding has occurred.

Application of international standards. Four African countries have reported to the Secretary General that they have issued new prison laws or regulations influenced by the United Nations Standard Minimum Rules for the Treatment of Prisoners (Botswana, Morocco, South Africa, Zambia), and four others have reported to him concerning their prison rules (Dahomey, Ghana, Kenya, Togo). No African correctional plan refers explicitly to the Standard Minimum Rules or gives any indication of aiming at their systematic implementation. It is known, however, that Egypt planned to reduce the proportion of its prisoners in high-security prisons in accordance with United Nations Congress recommendations[19]; and some other planned changes were at least implicitly in accord with the Rules, as for example references to separation among different categories of prisoners

---

18. A. Milner, ed., *African Penal Systems* (London: Rutledge, 1969).

19. Egypt, Ministry of the Interior, *Egyptian Prisons* (Cairo, 1960).

(Sudan, Togo) or to provision of work opportunities and aftercare.

Complicating factors. Some African governments have inherited mammoth prisons (Morocco). Others practice the dispersal rather than the concentration of prison population and tend therefore to plan investments in considerable numbers of small- or medium-sized institutions. This is often justified by the desire to avoid the cost and risk of transporting prisoners over large distances. One plan has added, "To reduce costs and to keep prisoners of similar cultural levels together, the policy is being adopted of holding prisoners in their own regions" (Sudan, 1961–71). Another plan comments on the transfer of prisoners to distant prisons: "Thus prisoners suffer penalties not intended by the courts, such as separation from their families and homes by complete loss of contact" (Botswana).[20] However justifiable this policy may be, it may contribute to local over-crowding; thus, one plan comments: "Since the prison population cannot be evenly distributed among the prison facilities available due to the prohibitive cost of transferring prisoners from outlying areas to the larger prisons, some prisons are underestablished while others are frequently grossly over-crowded."[21]

Some plans mention the lengthening of prison sentences as part of a policy of deterrence as one reason for requiring more accommodation (Kenya, Tanzania).

Some suggest an increase in female lawbreaking, to the point where women's prisons are needed (Lesotho, for 120 women;

20. Botswana, *National Development Plan, 1970–75* (Gaberone, 1970).

21. Botswana, *National Development Plan, 1968–1973* (Gaberone, 1968).

Kenya, regional women's prison; Uganda, 3 women's prisons) or at least a women's section (Sudan, Togo).

One speaks of an increase in mentally disturbed prisoners (Sudan: increase 203 to 521 between 1955 and 1961).

Most plans do not indicate to what extent the overcrowding of prisons may be due to the frequency of preventive detention while under trial, or the imprisonment of persons against whom the prosecution is not further pursued. One plan says, however: "The problem is complicated by the shortage of magistrates, which tends to increase figures for remand prisoners who must be kept in the prisons nearest to the courts in which they are tried."[22] Some plans include new remand prisons (Kenya, Uganda, 1966), or a new capital remand block for prisoners accused of murder (Kenya), or separation of under-trial from sentenced prisoners. It is known, however, that in several countries one half of the prison population may have been awaiting trial (Ivory Coast, Morocco, Nigeria), while in many countries in the course of a year more have been committed for safe custody than for imprisonment.

Nor do the plans give any indication to what extent imprisonment may have been due to inability to pay fines or to detention of witnesses.

As with police, one of the investments required in support of prisons has been housing for prison personnel. One plan remarks that the prison attendants were worse housed than the prisoners (Kenya), while another aims at accommodation for almost as many staff members as additional prisoners (Uganda, 1971: 2,000 and 3,000).

The one plan that indicates the number of prison personnel suggests a ratio of attendants to prisoners of 1:4, approximately

----

22. Uganda, *Work for Progress: Uganda's Second Development Plan, 1966–1971* (Kampala, 1966).

the same as in the United Kingdom (Uganda); and Kenya budgets for about this level. In Lesotho and Sierra Leone it has been 1:6; in Nigeria, 1:7; in Morocco, 1:10; and in Ivory Coast, 1:20. It is reported that there is often a shortage of rehabilitative personnel trained in education, health, and social work, and that in francophone countries no appropriate training has been developed for prison social work.

Classical approaches. What most African plans propose is to build more places of confinement (Ghana, Ivory Coast, Kenya, Nigeria, Uganda) or to enlarge existing ones.

Many also propose to improve the prisons by electrifying them, including security lighting, and by improving their drainage, waste disposal, and water supply, as well as by making them more secure.

Some have attempted diversification among their prisons, as by building additional "open" prisons (Ghana) or trying to draw off the prison population into corrective training centers for young adults, extramural penal employment, and short sentence camps (Kenya). A Kenya plan to reduce the pressure on the prisons proper did not prevent the total number of persons under custody from continuing to rise instead of falling according to plan (compare 1964 and 1966 plans).

Many plans include investment in prison workshops in order that prisoners may be taught a craft or engaged in useful work. They suggest that such opportunities, where they exist, may be available only to a few, but that an effort is being made to make them more widely available. One plan notes that it is government policy to insist that ministries place their orders with prison industries (Kenya, 1970–74). Another mentions earnings from the leasing of penal service (Madagascar, 1964).

There is great emphasis on the rehabilitative value of discipline, including in some countries the discipline of regular and useful work, as well as the value of self-support for self-respect, to the point where one administrator has reported: "We have now achieved full and useful employment for all inmates" (Kenya).[23]

One plan, concerned with aftercare of prisoners, commented: "The situation is not too bad for the prisoners from rural areas who can return to their land and cattle, but there is a great deal of recidivism among prisoners from the towns." It therefore proposed prison welfare officers to help prison-leavers into employment (Botswana, 1968). A subsequent plan, however, gave priority to making the prisons themselves more rehabilitative (1970).

When Nigeria integrated its federal, local government, and native administration prisons into a single national system, it seized the opportunity to regroup them on a functional basis into remand and reception centers, industrial production prisons, industrial training prisons, and prison farms, in line with an expert report on reorganization of the prison service (1970-74 plan).

Alternatives to institutional treatment. Because African development plans deal with investment projects rather than with overall policy, there may be important policy changes that pass without mention. Plans have thus had no occasion to refer to the widespread revival of both corporal and capital punishment. It is also unusual to find a plan that includes provision for the treatment of adult offenders in freedom. Nor do plans refer to the extent to which use is to be made of the provisions for restitution embodied in many African penal codes. There is, however, one which includes a project for noncustodial means

---

23. James M. Muturi, "Action-Research Basis of the Treatment of Offenders in Kenya," paper prepared for the Interregional Seminar on the Use of Research as a Basis for Social Defense Policy and Planning, Rungstedgaard, Denmark, 20-30 August 1973.

of treatment of offenders: "Government will explore alternative means for the treatment of offenders and will consider the extended use of such measures as probation, parole and suspended sentences. This will help to reduce the pressure on the prison structure."

Innovative correctional measures. While some countries have regarded their prisons as being so economically nonproductive that there is little point in investing scarce resources in their improvement (Ivory Coast), others have pioneered in ways of combining custodial care with outdoor economic activity. Beginning with extramural penal labor in Tanganyika in 1933, and soon extending also to the prison farm, this approach dominates the correctional component of the development plans of Eastern and Southern Africa.

The most radical of such solutions has been planned by Tanzania: "Prisons will also carry out a rehabilitation program for habitual criminals by resettling them in villages where they will be encouraged to engage in productive activities."[25] It is also known that Somalia has established cooperative villages for former habitual offenders and their families, besides settling them on state farms along with the urban unemployed.

Another possibility has been the use of prisoners on public works. Rhodesia plan, for example, has said: "Considerable thought has been given to long-term prison policies with particular emphasis on siting. Present thinking is that new expenditure should be devoted to small, minimum- and medium-security prisons in rural areas which can be constructed cheaply and which will enable prisoners to be usefully employed on

24. Lesotho, *First Five-Year Development Plan, 1970/71 to 1974/75* (Maseru, 1970).

25. Tanzania, *Second Five-Year Plan for Economic and Social Development 1969–74* (Dar-es-Salaam 1969).

Government projects in the vicinity."[26] The Lesotho courts, on the other hand, have been empowered to give first offenders sentenced to short terms for minor offenses the option of extramural employment on public facilities. The most widespread of distinctively African practices has become the prison farm. Botswana's plans moved rapidly from public works to agricultural camps:

> At present prisons are overcrowded . . . and there are no resources available for the rehabilitation of prisoners. One way in which the prison population may be decreased will be through the introduction of an extramural labour scheme. Instead of receiving prison sentences, offenders will be attached to local authorities for whom they will have to work in return for rations. Due to this scheme any increase in the number of offenders will not create a proportional demand for funds by the Prison Department.[27]

It is very desirable not only to alleviate overcrowding in prisons but also to ensure that stock thieves and other unsophisticated lawbreakers do not come into contact with hardened criminals. The most economical way of achieving these objects is by establishing prison camps for first offenders. The capital costs of the camps would be roughly half that of providing equivalent conventional facilities. Recurrent costs would also be lower. The camps will be sited either adjacent to Agricultural Department

---

26. Rhodesia, *Development Plan* (Salisbury, 1965).

27. Botswana, *Development Plan* (Gaberone, 1966).

49

farms or in other areas where crops can be grown for sale.[28]

In shifting the balance of its correctional system from urban prisons to rural farms, Kenya has planned to make its prison population self-supporting. Its plan states that every prison, however small, has at least its own vegetable garden.[29] Lesotho has planned three open prisons for first or minor offenders, with opportunity for market gardening and animal husbandry, adding:

> Recurrent expenditure on prisons should not be increased by this programme. Net revenue from prison industries and farms should increase (or the cost of feeding prisoners be reduced) by the provision of more funds for prison industries and the establishment of open prisons.[30]

Sudan's plan for the 1960s said:

> Prison industries and farms have expanded rapidly, contributing S£ 44,015 in prison revenue (1960/61) compared with S£ 8,069 (1955/56). Further development is required in order to increase the self-sufficiency of prisons in foodstuffs, clothing, etc. and to provide constructive employment for prisoners.[31]

---

28. Botswana, *National Development Plan, 1968–1973* (Gaberone, 1968). Repeated in Botswana, *National Development Plan, 1970–75* (Gaberone, 1970) on farm camps for rural first offenders.

29. Kenya, *Development Plan for the Period 1970 to 1974* (Nairobi, 1969).

30. Lesotho, *First Five-Year Development Plan, 1970/71—1974/75* (Maseru, 1970).

31. Sudan, *Ten-Year Plan of Economic and Social Development, 1961/62—1970/71* (Khartoum, 1962).

Tanzania plans farms to grow tea, tobacco, rice, and wheat among other things; its current plan says:

Considerable expansion of farming activities, according to crop priorities worked out by Kilimo (Ministry of Agriculture), is expected during the Plan and it will be necessary to engage farm managers in the bigger farms which cannot be managed by prison staff. Most development funds will go into building of staff quarters and to provide agricultural inputs for the farming activities.[32]

Uganda's plan stated:

During the First Plan (1961/1966) five prison farms were built, with accommodation for 2800 prisoners. These have proved successful, and more are to be built. The basic principle of prison farms is that the institutional treatment of offenders must be integrated with the development of the economy. Uganda being a country with abundant agricultural land, the rehabilitative programmes should train prisoners in modern methods of agriculture so that after discharge they can return to their homes and earn an honest living from their own pieces of land. Furthermore, prisoners represent a considerable labour force, which should be utilized in productive ways to offset some of the costs of maintaining the Prison Service.[33]

By 1970, half of Uganda's prisoners were on prison farms built since independence.[34]

---

32. Tanzania, *Second Five-Year Plan for Economic and Social Development, 1969–1974* (Dar-es-Salaam, 1969).

33. Uganda, *Work for Progress: Uganda's Second Five-Year Plan, 1966–1971* (Kampala, 1966).

34. *International Review of Criminal Policy,* No. 29 (1971), p. 97 (United Nations publication, Sales No. 72.IV.2).

d. Juvenile Delinquency Prevention

Dimensions of the problem. The transformation of traditional ways of life has brought with it the appearance of considerable numbers of children without families. According to the development plans, the Tunisian children who pass through the 26 "Bourguiba communities" established between 1956 and 1965 have numbered up to 6,000 at any time, out of a population of about 800,000 aged 5-14, while additional communities have been planned for an additional 1,200 children (1966). Wards of the state in the Somali Democratic Republic seem to number about 1 percent of the child population. In Kenya about 1,070 juveniles are confined by court decision, compared with about 500,000 boys aged 12-15 (1967). In the Sudan 398 were adjudged delinquent in 1960-61, up from 228 in 1955-56. Ethiopia's plan speaks of the Ministry of National Community Development's urban programs concentrating mainly on "the prevention of delinquency among the most vulnerable youth, about 4,000 homeless boys," by relying on bilaterally assisted voluntary associations and institutions, although there were actually only 138 boys committed to a center built for 100 (1963). In Morocco about 1,000 in 1 million boys aged 10-14 have been reported as being in observation or reeducation centers or hostels under the Ministry of Youth and Social Affairs.

It is known from United Nations studies that in Egypt in 1963, the police prosecuted more than 24,000 offenses by juveniles in a population of about 2.4 million boys aged 7-14, i.e., 10 per 1,000; that in Zambia in 1962, convictions were obtained against 1,100 Africans aged 12-16 out of about 167,000 boys in that age group, i.e., 6.6 per 1,000, and that in South Africa the conviction rate approached 100 per 1,000 in 1958.[35] In Zambia also, the daily average population in the reformatory was nearly 200,

---

35. *International Review of Criminal Policy,* No. 21 (1963), p. 24 (United Nations publication, Sales No. 64.IV.3.).

but for a somewhat greater age range, suggesting a ratio of about 1 per 1,000 in the male juvenile population.

Complicating factors. In the case of many of these children, it is hard to distinguish between neglect and delinquency, especially where vagrancy is an offense or the same juvenile court deals with neglect and disobedience as well as lawbreaking. They are spoken of in some French-language plans as *déshérités*; and others speak of predelinquents as well as delinquents. The Uganda plan has spoken of them as "children who are beyond parental control" and has added, "it is important that they should be retrieved before they drift, as they often do, into criminality."[36] In Egypt prosecutions for vagrancy alone have varied between 3 (1963) and 7 (1961) per 1,000 boys in the 7–14 age group.[37] A United Nations technical assistance adviser found in 1964 that very few of the boys committed to the training center at Addis Ababa had committed serious crimes.

Girls as well as boys are becoming a problem. Kenya has therefore planned a female probation hostel and a girls' corrective school.

Planned solutions. The plans give evidence of three principal African approaches to the problem of the child who grows up without a family. All tend to spring from a ministry of social affairs rather than from a ministry responsible for law and order, except in the Somali Democratic Republic.

One approach looks to treatment in the community. In anglophone countries this has been built around a probation service, envisaged in Africa as promoters of responsibility on the part of family members and voluntary agencies, rather than as direct supervisors of delinquents under court order. In some countries it turns on direct relations between the police and

---

36. Uganda, *Work for Progress: Uganda's Second Development Plan, 1966–1971* (Kampala, 1966).

37. United Nations study, SOA/SD/CS.1, 1966.

judiciary and the family. In either case it does not figure largely in African development plans, because its cost would fall more on the recurrent operating budgets than on capital outlay; but Nigeria (North) and Tanzania have included some small capital outlay for probation officers' offices and housing, and it seems that Uganda may have been considering additional recurrent outlay in its ordinary budget in order to more than double the number of its probation officers.[38] We know, however, from previous United Nations studies that supervised probation has reached a significant minority of juvenile delinquents in some countries, e.g., 16 percent in Zambia, and also that about 45 percent of juvenile delinquents in Egypt were "delivered to their families" in 1962, while in Zambia as many may have been bound over or warned as were placed under supervision.

A second approach, more frequently represented in development plans, has been to invest in the construction of additional residential institutions. Rhodesia's plan has thus stated that "existing facilities for African juveniles are fully extended" and therefore proposed extension of "probation hostels, remand homes and reformatories for Africans" (1965).

Among these congregate institutions many have been planned for children who need care but have not been adjudged delinquent. Some are permanent, such as the government orphanage for 600 boys sent from all over the country by local civil administrators, as well as two homes for several hundred handicapped children who might otherwise become beggars, reported by the Somali Democratic Republic. Others are temporary shelters for homeless children. Most are short-term observation centers, a considerable increase in the supply of which has been planned. For example, Kenya included five juvenile remand

---

38. *International Review of Criminal Policy,* No. 24 (1966), p. 78 (United Nations publication, Sales No. 67.IV.22).

homes in its first plan (1966) and later had nine with an average daily population of 160 (1970). Three observation centers planned by Tanzania for 1964-69 were still in the planning stage for 1969-74, although they were scaled down from 40 children each to 15 boys and 8 girls. Uganda had two remand homes and proposed to open four more (1966). Togo planned a reception center for juvenile vagrants and delinquents, where they could stay a few months while being reoriented (1966). Ethiopia planned to reorganize a voluntary agency "training center and remand home" for boys and to supplement it with one or two government homes (1963); and it requested United Nations technical assistance in this one aspect of social defense (1964).

Plans have also provided for additional corrective schools for adolescents adjudged delinquent. Thus, Chad and Benin have planned new "juvenile reeducation centers" and the Central African Republic a "home for delinquent children" (1965). Kenya planned two additional corrective schools under its first plan (1964), and later had eight—either junior (primary) or senior (vocational)—with an average daily population of 910 (1970); the children were to be kept in their own regions and at the same time the cost of transportation was kept down.

A third approach in some African countries has been particularly striking: it is the institution of children's villages, including an effort to enable adolescents to contribute collectively toward their own subsistence. The "Bourguiba communities" of Tunisia have already been mentioned; their expansion by five additional villages was planned to cost D.50,000 each (1966). The Somali Democratic Republic planned a "boys' village" for 200 vagrant boys aged 7-17 from Mogadishu as a pilot farm and training project, and a "revolutionary school" in each of its fourteen provinces to rear children who lack paternal support. The first of these settlements has been reported to have 2,000 residents. Tanzania plans nine "probation villages" "to accommodate delinquents on probation, who will be under the close supervision and guidance of probation staff, so that they can be finally assimilated in the community."[39]

In Africa, the most distinctive and innovative regional approaches to the treatment of homeless or delinquent youth have thus been their binding-over to the care of kinsfolk or, if they have no kinsfolk available to care for them, their settlement in substitute communities, with the former being generally excluded from and the latter included in the development plan.

B. ASIA AND THE FAR EAST

1. COMPREHENSIVE PLANNING IN RELATION TO CRIMINAL POLICY

a. Degrees of Inclusion or Exclusion
of Crime Control in Investment plans
Comprehensive inclusion of crime control facilities. Among Asian countries from which general national plans are currently available to the United Nations, only three have included all aspects of criminal policy: Burma (1961/65), Malaysia (1966/70), and Philippines (1971/74).

Burma allocated 11.5 percent of its public sector investment to what it called "law and order," with the comment, "Although the absolute level of capital expenditures on Law and Order is only slightly lower than in the previous periods (the 1950s) its relative share registers a significant decline on account of the larger base." It had in fact declined from 20 percent during the previous four years, these ratios being among the highest in the world. It is not clear, however, what was included by the plan under this heading. Detailed breakdowns for policing alone, including frontier areas administration, amounted to about 3.4

---

39. Tanzania, *Second Five-Year Plan for Economic and Social Development, 1st July 1969 to 30th June 1974* (Dar-es-Salaam, 1969–70).

percent of planned public sector capital outlays; and, in introducing this chapter, the plan stated:

Law and Order is the prerequisite of economic and social development. Development measures directed at the restoration of transport and communication, increased agricultural production, social services, electric power and industry, can be achieved best only when peaceful conditions obtain. The plan places great importance upon the maintenance of law and order.[40]

Malaysia raised its allocation for "internal security" from 3 percent of capital expenditures in 1961-65 to 4 percent of greatly increased public sector planned investments for the late 1960s with the comment:

. . . Defence and internal security expenditures will be 138 percent more. This vast increase in planned defence and internal security expenditure has been made necessary by the need of the country to withstand military confrontation.[41]

Among Oceanian countries, Fiji includes investment in police, courts, corrective schools, and prisons in its development planning, and has revised its current plan upwards in these respects.

Selective inclusion of social defense facilities. On the other hand, a considerable number of Asian plans include what they call "social defense" in only a narrow sense, excluding such essential aspects of criminal policy as police, courts, and

---

40. Burma, Ministry of National Planning, *Second Four-Year Plan for the Union of Burma, 1961-62 to 1964-65* (Rangoon, 1960).

41. Malaysia, *First Malaysian Plan, 1966-1970* (Kuala Lumpur, 1965).

prisons. In these instances it is envisaged as a subdivision of social welfare:

SOCIAL SERVICES SECTOR

SOCIAL WELFARE SUBSECTOR

Social Defense Subsubsector

The emphasis is here placed on the building up of constructive and preventive institutions as essential and innovative aspects of social development, rather than on the protective framework indispensable to all development, except insofar as the Philippine plan has prefaced its chapter on social welfare and manpower policy with this statement: "Economic development becomes meaningful when the broad base of the population is able to enjoy a decent level of living, and social order prevails."[42]

The proportion of planned public sector investment allocated to social defense in this restricted sense is extremely small, and seems usually to have been well below 1 percent of development outlay in the few countries for which quantitative estimates are available (Pakistan, 1965/70; Thailand, 1961/66) and to have declined from one plan to the next before almost disappearing (India, 1956/60, 1968/69, 1969/74; Sri Lanka, 1959/69, 1966/67, 1972/76).

Plans of Iran (1968/72), the Philippines (1962/67), and South Vietnam (1962/66), which also belong to this group, do not permit even the roughest quantitative estimates. They are nevertheless important as symbols of a preventive and rehabilitative philosophy rather than a deterrent and punitive approach to criminal policy. The work governed by such a philosophy may

---

42. Philippines, *Four-Year Development Plan, 1972-1975* (Manila, 1971).

be carried on by a ministry of social services rather than the old-line ministries mainly responsible for criminal policy. This may be one reason why this kind of preventive and rehabilitative approach is not explicitly stated in the plans of countries where social services are the responsibility of the same ministry as police and prisons (Thailand), or where the ministries of the interior and of justice have themselves become influenced by a preventive and rehabilitative approach (Japan).

One example of this insertion of a social service approach in a general development plan is Iran where the Ministry of Labor and Social Affairs has planned "rehabilitative services for specific socially handicapped groups," to be put at the disposal of the Department General of Prisons and, on behalf of addicts, of the Ministry of Health. At the planning level Iran thus has a certain interdepartmental coordination, although there is no evidence of criminal policy as a whole being planned.

Another example is Bangladesh, where social services for delinquents were transferred to a directorate of social welfare in accordance with two successive plans (1960/65, 1965/70) which recommended, not the coordinated control of all crime and delinquency, but the coordination of "the entire work in the field of social welfare," implying that their principle of administrative organization was the grouping of services not by function but by skill (in this case, social work)—and not counterbalancing this division of administrative responsibility with an organ for integrated planning.

Given the piecemeal approach of these plans to criminal policy, it is not surprising that some have included certain social welfare goals without analyzing or specifying the means that would be needed for achieving them. For example, India's first two plans had allocated more than R.80 million for changing the behavior patterns of "ex-criminal [later, "denotified"] tribes," before relegating the problem to the states with the comment, "Due to special difficulties . . . viz. stigma of criminality . . . it has not been possible to tackle the problem of rehabilitating these groups successfully.''[43] The eradication of beggary has similarly proved beyond the immediate means of many of the governments that have endorsed the principle in their development plans but have not had the personnel or machinery for applying the principle on a more than local scale. Much the same could be said of plan endorsements of the extension of criminal legislation into such fields as prostitution and the abuse of alcohol. Planning to meet and, where possible forestall, these social problems has been of limited value because it has neglected to take fully into account their relationship to all aspects of criminal policy and the burden that dealing with them would impose on the police and on correctional treatment.

Omission of criminal justice from development plan. A third group of countries comprises those whose development plans completely omit any reference to criminal policy, either because the plans are purely economic in a narrow sense, or because the only aspects of social development which they include relate to human resources as a factor of production. These include Cambodia (1960-64), China (Taiwan, 1960-72), Indonesia (1956/60, 1969/74), Japan (1964/69), Korea (1962-66, 1967/71), Laos (1959/64), Mongolia (1966-70), Nepal (1965/70/75), and Sri Lanka (1972-76). It is of course not impossible that some non-specified crime control outlays may buried among capital outlays on administrative infrastructure where these are included; but Nepal explicitly excludes them.

b. The Place of Criminal Policy in Operating Budgets

The budgets of countries in Asia and the Far East reveal that in the developed countries of the region the operating cost of criminal justice, as in other regions, represents about 3 percent of total recurrent governmental expenditures (Australia, Japan), but that in the less developed countries it is higher, approaching

43. India, Planning Commission, *Fourth Five-Year Plan, 1966-1971* (New Delhi, 1966).

10 percent in countries exposed to heavy internal security risks.[44] A review of the national budgets indicates also that the expansion of criminal justice outlays may have been less rapid than that of governmental expenditures in general during the 1960s (India, Indonesia, Pakistan).

Development plans in this region are not much concerned with commitments to the recurring costs of criminal justice. The Philippines are nevertheless among the countries in which it has been planned to expand expenditure on internal order relatively as well as absolutely. A four-year national fiscal budget (1968) allocated about 7.5 percent of general fund expenditure to the constabulary, the courts, and the prisons. A recent development plan (1971-74) reckons outlay on "maintenance of peace and order" and "administration of justice" at a little over 10 percent of combined national and local expenditures and foresees a growth two or three times as rapid in these areas as in other expenditures.

2. EXTENT OF INTEGRATED PLANNING IN THE CRIMINAL POLICY SECTOR

No Asian plan, any more than others, offers any evidence of integrated planning of criminal policy as a distinct and coherent system. In Burma, all the planned capital outlays are grouped under the heading "civil works." In Malaysia they are scattered under "internal security" (police), "general administration" (courthouses, prisons), and "welfare services" (juvenile delinquency). Outside their plans, however, Japan and Singapore have provided model quantitative analyses of the whole criminal justice process.[45]

---

44. See table, p. 114.

45. United Nations Asia and Far East Institute for the Prevention of Crime and Treatment of Offenders (UNAFEI), *Report for 1970,* and *Resource Material Series, No. 1,* March 1971 and No. 6, October 1973.

In India the states have divided responsibilities among home departments for police, inspectors general for prisons, and directorates of welfare for treatment of offenders. At the center, the Planning Commission has occasionally set up a limited program-planning group, such as a committee of inquiry on prohibition for the second plan, or a study group on eradication of beggary from tourist centers, places of pilgrimage and big cities, in preparation for the fourth plan. India's second, third, and annual plans included provision for the social welfare "growing edges" of corrections, by way of earmarked 50:50 grants to the states; but the recent fourth plan leaves priorities to the states. Meanwhile, responsibility for central standard-setting through the new Central Bureau of Correctional Services was transferred from the Home Affairs to the Social Welfare Ministry.

In a few rare instances most aspects of criminal justice administration come under a single ministry (Pakistan, Thailand); and this may give rise to some innovative interaction between the various component elements (see Thailand, p. 69).

Outside of general development plans there has arisen in a few countries an official organ able to view criminal justice as a whole. In India, this is done to some extent by the Central Bureau of Correctional Services through its quarterly periodical, *Social Defence*. In Japan it is done by the Research and Training Institute of the Ministry of Justice through its annual *White Paper on Crime: Trends in Crime and Problems relating to the Treatment of Offenders* (English summaries, 1963, 1969).

The United Nations Asia and Far East Institute for the Prevention of Crime and Treatment of Offenders has helped attract attention toward the planning of the criminal justice system as a whole, especially by disseminating the techniques of the flow chart showing the paths followed by offenders as they move through the system. (UNAFEI, *Report for 1971 and Resource Material Series No. 3*, Fuchu, Tokyo 1972).

3. SUBSECTORAL PLANNING PROBLEMS

a. Law Enforcement Planning.

Dimensions of the problem. One Asian plan specifies the size of its state police forces as part of its plan for social insurance (Iran). From other countries the size of the police forces is known mainly from annual budgetary documents and reports. As everywhere, many number about two agents per 1,000 population; but the frequency of lower ratios suggests heavy use of police substitutes.

Here as elsewhere, there have been fluctuations in the offenses known to the police, sometimes with marked declines followed by rises, but with a notable increase in the load of work arising from lawbreaking without criminal intent, connected generally with the spread of the automobile. In this region the experience of Japan suggests that the number of persons in prison can be reduced, regardless of what happens to the number of offenses known to the police.

Classical development envisaged. Burma's plan has included detailed programs for mitigating the effects of the assignment of the police force to the suppression of insurgency and other internal security measures, by strengthening it for suppression of crime. Expansion of "order work" was to be achieved by continuous patrolling of rural areas with modern road and water equipment, extension of day- and night-patrol from the capital to other cities; possible transfer of anti-insurgency outposts to the armed forces; opening of more ordinary police stations as security improved (41 planned for 1961); improvement of surveillance by revival of criminal records destroyed during the war and insurrections; systematic enforcement of public discipline, traffic, excise, and gambling regulations; and arrest of absconders. Expansion of "crime work" was to include reduction of investigative officers' work load to 75 cases a year and development of a prosecuting cadre so that cases might be better presented to the courts and fewer cases lost. The plan also contained a program for qualitative improvement by training courses, including training of officers to give in-service training to their subordinates and attendance of senior officers at the national defense college, and also by morale-lifting measures such as increased salaries, welfare facilities, public relations, and advisory committees. The four-year capital outlay program was for modernization and construction of lockups, officers' quarters, radio stations, police stations, medico-legal institutes, pathological laboratories, garages, office and supply buildings, as well as purchase of vehicles, watercraft, equipment, and stores. Maintenance of security in frontier areas had already been transferred by the states to the union government in 1959.

The Malaysian plan has indicated that over two thirds of its investment in "internal security" could go for police accommodation.

Popular participation in policing. No Asian development plan has been found to contain a program designed to increase the effectiveness of a police force by supplementing it with part-time citizen reserves.

It is known, however, that in many countries of Eastern and Southern Asia the size of the regular police force is kept down, outside the plan, by traditional reliance on self-policing by rural communities and by extension of this practice to urban neighborhoods. In some Indian states, for example, paid police are supplemented with village volunteer forces, and many minor offenses are handled through local community organs rather than being reported to a police station. Japan reports 125,000 "cooperators for juvenile guidance" commissioned by the prefects to work with police patrols (UNAFEI, 1970, p. 130). South Korea has reported that 5,000 volunteers in a citizens' crime prevention corps were assisting in night patrol where local police forces were insufficient in size to prevent crimes effectively. Hong Kong and Singapore have reported organized public participation in preventive policing as a reserve of special constables.

b. Judicial Policy

No one reading East Asian development plans would guess that many countries in that region are actively pursuing policies of developing institutions for settling disputes without recourse to professionally staffed law courts. These policies require no planned investments and involve little or no additional budget expenditure.

In its concentration on "hardware" rather than on "software," all that a development plan usually indicates is the building of new courthouses or the replacement of old ones. This may be very important in a country such as Afghanistan, where for the first time the central government's court system is reaching out into the provinces, with the building of judicial compounds as well as courthouses (1967–71).

It is well known, however, that Indian government policy has promoted *nyaya panchayats*, through which many disputes have been handled by local people's tribunals, and that neighboring countries have adopted similar policies. In Sri Lanka the police and the courts have promoted local arbitral councils (*gan sabha*) of prominent citizens commissioned by the Ministry of Justice. Nepal has its local *panchayats*. In Bangladesh, union councils have set up conciliation courts including nominees of the parties. Beneath the classical court system, and outside the plan, Iran has developed official popular tribunals composed of unpaid elective judges: "houses of equity" in the villages since 1963 and arbitral councils in urban quarters since 1966; they are elected by their constituents, and their decisions are final if they are agreed to by the parties and the local justice of the peace does not disagree. In Taiwan, every rural township has its mediation committee, where decisions become final with consent of the parties and approval of a judge. In general, these local popular tribunals have been authorized to handle only minor disputes and to prevent their developing into major ones, and have been empowered to award compensation but not to inflict penalties.

To settle major disputes, lay assessors sitting with a

professional magistrate have been preferred, an extreme example on the northwest frontier of Pakistan being the revival of traditional *jirgas* for trying serious offenses where four respectable local citizens selected by the civil administrator and sitting with a magistrate were given wide latitude to act on evidence that was satisfactory by local customary standards, but not by those of the ordinary law courts.

Japan has introduced lay local "inquest committees" empowered to review the public procurator's decision not to prosecute, if requested by the original complainant or victim.

In addition to this wide-scale promotion of popular participation in the judicial process, other alternatives to hearings before trial courts have also been developed. Thus, Japan reports that it has given minor violators and traffic offenders the opportunity to be dealt with summarily without public hearings; more than 4 million cases were reported handled in this way in 1967.

Going outside the system of civilian courts, it is also known that Iran has extended military jurisdiction to cases of highway robbery, armed bank robbery, and illegal drug traffic.

c. Treatment of Offenders

Dimensions of the problem. Only the Fijian plan offers an estimate of the dimensions of the need for prisons or other forms of correctional care.

From other official sources, it is known, however, that the fraction of the population that is imprisoned in the regular course of criminal justice remains relatively low—which may be one of the reasons why outlay on prisons is seldom included in Asian development plans.

It is also known that the fraction of the population that is confined to prison has tended to decline in some Asian countries, whether this be measured by committals in the course of a year or by occupancy on a given day; the most striking example of this decline is Japan, where the proportion of the population in prison has fallen dramatically from 1.2 per 1,000 in 1950 to 0.5 in 1972.

Overcrowding of prisons is nevertheless reported from some countries. Almost everywhere it is related to the fact that more persons are remanded into custody while awaiting trial than are sentenced to imprisonment after conviction. In India overcrowding has been sometimes linked also to short sentences and prohibition offenses, as well as to the possibility that population increases may have outrun increases in prison capacity; and it may have been a stimulus to various measures to alleviate overcrowding, such as opening of prison farms and release of prisoners on parole. In Sri Lanka it has been attributed to inability to pay fines. In Japan, on the other hand, severe overcrowding during the postwar crime epidemic is reported now to have been almost overcome.

Application of international standards. No Asian plan is couched in terms of implementation of the United Nations Standard Minimum Rules for the Treatment of Prisoners. A previous study has indicated, however, that New Zealand and Singapore have issued new prison regulations influenced by the Rules; that India, Japan and Thailand have issued official translations of the Rules; and that in India the central Ministry of Home Affairs has issued an All-India Model Prison Manual which it recommended in 1964 for possible adoption by the states.[45a]

Complicating factors. In Asian countries there has been some tendency toward extension of the scope of the criminal law, rather than decriminalization; this has been reflected in planning for specialized services in respect of some forms of social behavior that were formerly condoned or cultivated. Many countries have made begging a punishable offense (Burma, In-

---

45a. *International Review of Criminal Policy*, No. 26, 1968, page 74 (United Nations publication, Sales No.: 70.IV.1).

dia, Iran, Pakistan, Sri Lanka, Vietnam). This has required preventive action in the form of public aid in place of private charity and remedial action by way of special institutions for reception, training, and employment of beggars. Most Asian plans therefore include programs for expansion of beggars' homes or work centers, even though the measures planned may in some instances constitute only token recognition of a principle (for example, 16 for Pakistan under its third plan or 14 in India at the end of the third plan). A similar situation has arisen with legislation making prostitution in all its forms an offense (as with the Suppression of Immoral Traffic Acts of Burma, India, Iran, and Pakistan), going much further than was required by ratification of the United Nations convention against the exploitation of the prostitution of others. This has led to planned support for rehabilitation centers for prostitutes, even if only on a token scale (Burma, India, Iran, Malaysia, Pakistan). India's second plan included also a program for state prohibition of alcoholic beverages; and this required not only prosecution and imprisonment of violators but also planned outlay on publicity campaigns in support of prohibition, until the policy was eventually dropped as being impractical except for the educational component.

A serious planning problem has arisen in the most populous Asian country with a federal constitution, owing to the devolution of responsibility for criminal justice on to the component states, although the criminal code was of central origin. India held its eighth and last conference of state inspectors general of prisons in 1952 in connection with a United Nations technical assistance mission. Central standard-setting and information exchange were subsequently placed on a continuing basis under an All-India Jail Manual Committee (1957–60), Central Bureau of Correctional Services (from 1961), and Central Advisory Board on Correctional Services (from 1969); and this last has recently begun to bring together representatives of Union ministries of home affairs, law, and social welfare as well as selected state inspectors general of prisons and some academic experts. On the other hand, few federal incentives to state implementation of standards have been available, by way either of development plan allocations or of operational grants-in-aid.

Relation of planning to corrections. One radical way of involving corrections into broader development processes has been illustrated by Thailand, where the Ministry of the Interior is responsible for community development as well as for prisons and police. Of its effort to make lawbreakers self-supporting by absorbing prisoner rehabilitation into land settlement, a Thai plan has said: "The self-help land settlement project aims at assisting people who are without land to acquire cultivable land and to settle down peacefully as respectable cultivators of the soil. This is one of the measures taken to further the prevention of crime."[46]

Traditional obstacles to any major inclusion of custodial institutions in a development plan have been illustrated by the Indian submission to the Fourth United Nations Congress on the Prevention of Crime and the Treatment of Offenders (Kyoto, 1970), which stated:

There is a strong demand which has been often expressed, that the prison administration, which is outside the Plan Sector, should be brought into the Plan. It is also felt that agriculture, industries, education and other activities carried out within the walls of the prisons should be treated as sectors of General Plan Progress Programme eligible for development funds. It has, however, been seen that there is a considerable resistance, presumably based on inadequate information, to treat prisons as a part of the Plan. Under

---

46. Thailand, National Economic Development Board, *National Economic Development Plan, 1964–1966* (Bangkok, 1964).

these circumstances, the prison administration does not share the benefit of the development programme. This has led to a stagnation and sense of frustration amongst correctional administrators. This is, perhaps, a reflection of the general apathy on behalf of the public which is reflected in the attitude of policy-makers. It only goes to show that greater efforts are necessary to create a better public understanding of the issues involved in the correctional process.

Previously, however, India had made a modest effort to use development planning as a lever for modifying the orientation of the correctional process:

The Central Government has also suggested that in States where a probation system does not already exist, a beginning should now be made. It is further proposed that in the more important jails welfare officers should be appointed for the purpose of contacting prisoners during their stay in jails and for keeping in touch with them and their families after release.[47]

Such small sums as were formerly earmarked for this program (1956–69) are reported to have resulted in the number of state probation officers being doubled during this time to nearly 400 (one per 1.25 million population), into whose supervision about 14,000 persons were released. The number of state prison welfare officers, on the other hand, remained low, with case loads nearer to 2,000 than to the 200 recommended; and a decline in voluntary aftercare associations has been reported. The small plan allocations available for these social welfare services were underspent and discontinued (1969).

---

47. India, *Second Five-Year Plan* (New Delhi, 1956).

Besides these infrequent but distinctive cases, Asia also illustrates the planning of capital investment in prisons in relation to differential land values. This is exemplified by the Malaysian plan which included provision for additional prison accommodation and staff quarters, both in Malaya and in the Borneo states; the biggest item was linked to the redevelopment of the heart of the federal capital, where a valuable area was to be freed by rebuilding a prison outside the city.

Correctional policy outside the development plans. The development plans of Asian countries give little indication of the important developments which may nevertheless be occurring in the treatment of offenders.

The progress made by some countries in reducing the incidence of imprisonment has been accompanied by increased treatment in the community. Japan now has more persons on probation than in prison, thanks to nearly 50,000 volunteer counselors organized in local associations by 500 professional probation supervisors. In Japan the number of fines has also exceeded the number of sentences of imprisonment since 1955; in the following ten years the number of fines increased by 200 percent while that of imprisonments declined by 30 percent.

Local popular participation in the correctional process is reported also from South Korea, where a civic rehabilitation agency organized 1,200 volunteer counselors and from Taiwan where an aftercare association grouped 4,000 volunteer guidance officers.[48]

Outside the plan, Iran has taken steps to keep down the use of penal institutions, particularly by authorizing suspended sentences (1967) and conditional release (1958, etc.), and by establishing a standing penal reform commission in the Ministry

---

48. United Nations Asia and Far East Institute for the Prevention of Crime and the Treatment of Offenders (UNAFEI), *Resource Material Series* No. 2 (November, 1971).

of Justice.

Sri Lanka introduced "release on license" for long-term prisoners in 1969.

South Korea has reported a Reformative Construction Corps through which 120,000 ablebodied offenders worked on road, reclamation, and other public works projects during three years (1967–70).

Recognition of the inappropriateness of imprisonment for many offenders is illustrated by a Pakistani report in justification of probation:

> Today in Pakistan over 70 percent of the total population in jails consists of those raw and chance offenders in whose cases the terms of sentence range from one month or less to one year. Generally these cases are of those persons who have landed themselves behind the bars as a result of a fight over land or water or due to some family feuds or disputes. And most of them are devoid of any criminal characteristics—their contamination with confirmed criminals and professionals in jail only harms them rather than doing any good to them. (Lahore, 1961)

Open prisons, although less typical of this region than high-security institutions, have been studied by the United Nations Asia and Far East Institute.[49] Two penal systems keep one third of the convicted prisoners in small, open, rural prisons used for men serving short sentences (Sri Lanka, Hong Kong). Another country has one third of its prisoners in large open penal colonies where long-term prisoners can be assigned immediately

49. United Nations Asia and Far East Institute for the Prevention of Crime and Treatment of Offenders (UNAFEI), *The Open Correctional Institution in Asia and the Far East* (New York: United Nations, 1965 [TAO/AFE/14]).

after classification (Philippines). Some other countries have tried to decongest overcrowded prisons without building new ones, by developing satellite work camps or prison farms to which men can be assigned during the concluding stage of long-term imprisonment (Indian States, Japan).

In some countries the criminal law provides for administrative detention without trial of members of organizations believed capable of violently preventing the operation of normal judicial processes. This may make heavy demands on correctional facilities, as in Singapore where one third of the prisoners are detained as nonconvicted members of secret societies in addition to almost as many other members who are under police supervision in their homes. Burma has reported 1,000 detainees in 1966 and Malaysia 1,500 in 1971.

The correctional processes whose development is considered here are those which operate in a continuing and predictable manner. They do not include such unplanned deprivation of freedom as has occurred in times of emergency, when large numbers of persons believed to be politically dangerous have sometimes been detained without previous establishment of a procedure for civil review of individual cases.

d. Juvenile Delinquency Services

Dimensions of the problem. India's second plan stated that juvenile delinquency had been growing in large cities, the most common offense being theft. From a study made for the United Nations it is known that police apprehensions at that time for cognizable offenses had reached 2 in Delhi and 2.8 in Calcutta for 1,000 boys aged 12-16, while apprehensions for non-cognizable offenses were estimated at as many again.[50] Japan reports a rate of 2 per 1,000 boys of that age range sent to the procurator in 1970, down from 3.5 five years earlier, although

---

50. United Nations study, SOA/SD/CS.2, 1967.

cases referred to a family court were nine times as numerous as at the earlier date.

Much juvenile lawbreaking has of course consisted of petty violations, but has exposed the violators to different treatment from that accorded to adults insofar as it has indicated a lack of parental authority and has therefore elicited a countervailing desire to substitute public authority. Much also has consisted of grown-up behavior considered improper in persons who are still growing up.

As everywhere, the problem has not been confined to actual delinquency but has been extended to homeless or neglected children. Development plans indicate that Sri Lanka subsidized 90 voluntary agency homes for 5,500 children in 1970, and that India knew of 120 homes for 6,000 children in 1960. Thailand's plan speaks of training "orphans, homeless children, juvenile delinquents and other underprivileged or socially maladjusted youngsters."

Plan responses. India's Second Plan (1956/60) included the building up of a nucleus of essential state and voluntary institutions for combating juvenile delinquency, including promotion of appropriate legislation and courts:

> The Central Government has suggested to States that there should be a remand home in each important town in which juveniles in custody may be lodged during the period of investigation or trial. It has also suggested that each State should have a certified school and a hostel for boys, where juveniles released on probation can be lodged if they cannot be attached to suitable families during this period. Finally, each State should have a borstal school for young delinquents between the ages of 15 and 21 years. Child guidance clinics and school social workers could assist in early treatment of behaviour problems and in reducing the incidence of juvenile delinquency.

This resulted in a near doubling of the number of remand homes and of reeducation schools ("certified," "approved," "reformatory") in the next fifteen years; but, even so, their capacity reached only 6,000 in 100 remand homes and 12,000 in 100 schools. A recent plan (1969–74) notes the difficulty of spending plan monies on these and other social welfare activities when it is necessary to work through state authorities or voluntary agencies.

Iran planned to build 5 training and reform centers for 500 young delinquents, besides one recently established, as well as to revise its juvenile court law so as to introduce court social work and supervised probation, for which it proposed to train 30 court social workers and 30 probation supervisors.

A Pakistani plan said: "There are many adolescents and youths without healthy occupations in schools and colleges and in the community, who are forced by circumstances and opportunities to indulge in unsocial and immoral activities and who join gangs and racketeers, pickpockets and other similar groups." Federal funds offered through the previous plan had not been matched by the provinces. The need was estimated at 315 "service units" for about 31,500 young people, each unit including juvenile court, remand home, reeducation center, and probation service; but only 18 were projected for the third plan (1965–70).

Responses outside the plans. Some Asian plans, as we have seen, propose to strengthen the rehabilitative as against the punitive aspects of the classical Euramerican apparatus for handling juvenile delinquency.

On the hand, no plans propose to economize in public action by adopting the recommendation "that, even for protection, specific offences which would penalize small irregularities or maladjusted behaviour of minors, but for which adults would not be prosecuted, should not be created.''[51] On the contrary, there has been a tendency to conserve and enforce the traditional view that underage status is incompatible with such grown-up behavior as smoking or frequenting adult places of amusement. What is innovative is the development of new forms of authority for maintaining minor status.

Another tendency outside the plans and also in the realm of service rather than facilities, is the use of police authority in order to modify the behavior of juveniles. For example, Japan reports that the police gave ''guidance or direction'' to nearly one million juveniles (45 per 1,000) aged 8–19 in 1968, mainly for breaches of the status expected of juveniles in ways that would not have been unlawful in adults. Similar police roles are reported from China (Taiwan), Hong Kong, Korea, and Thailand.[52]

A third nonpunitive approach that requires little planned investment in facilities may be found in the practice of juvenile courts, in countries where they handle many cases, of disposing of most of them by using their authority to strengthen that of the families. It is thus reported that four fifths of all the cases that went before Japanese family courts in 1968 were dismissed before or after hearing; and, of the criminal cases, only one in ten was disposed of by probation, and one in forty by committal to an institution.

The seriousness with which government views the breakdown of family authority is illustrated by Japan's authorization of

---

51. *Report of the Second United Nations Congress on the Prevention of Crime and the Treatment of Offenders* (United Nations publication, Sales No. 61.IV.3).

52. United Nations Asia and Far East Institute for the Prevention of Crime and Treatment of Offenders (UNAFEI), *Comparative Survey of Juvenile Delinquency in Asia and the Far East,* by A. A. G. Peters (Fuchu, Tokyo, 1969).

preventive detention before trial in order to protect witnesses and complainants against juvenile groups.

C. LATIN AMERICA AND THE CARIBBEAN

1. COMPREHENSIVE PLANNING

a. Exclusion of Crime from Mainland
Development Plans in the 1960s
Most Latin American countries have development plans. Nevertheless, during the 1960s no development plan available from any independent country on the mainland included any investment in the protection of developmental resources and processes against lawbreaking. Most development plans included such aspects of social development as education, health, housing, social security, and community development, but no prevention of delinquency or treatment of offenders. Instead, they regarded "justice and police" as part of the traditional governmental overheads which were viewed as nonproductive and which should therefore have their rate of expansion slowed down. And most buried justice and police so completely under the heading "general government" that it is not possible to disentagle them. This approach was that not only of individual country plans but also of the Alliance for Progress and the Organization of American States.

b. Inclusion of Criminal Policy in
Mainland Development Plans for the 1970s
Recent development plans indicate a change, in the those for Argentina (1971/75), Brazil (1970), and Venezuela (1970–74) all contain proposals concerning justice or social defense, although none is explicit concerning projected investment outlays.
The Venezuelan plan for what it calls social defense is almost as broad   as the plan in its entirety. This is because of its

philosophic viewpoint. Instead of arguing a fiscal or economic case for including crime control in a development plan, it builds on the Latin American positivist tradition that looks outside the criminal justice system for the causes of crime:

> The concept of Social Defence starts from the supposition that offences against persons and groups are the result of the structural conditions characteristic of a society rather than of individual maladjustments. As a matter of fact, experience demonstrates that the raising of the level of living of the population, the increase in opportunities of employment and training, and a more satisfactory distribution of income, among other factors, contribute to improve the crime index.
>
> In its broader sense, the term Social Defence includes the appearance of new kinds of crime such as the violation of human rights, speculation and the destruction of the physical environment.
>
> A modern state ought to develop policies intended to prevent crime before it turns into a criminal act subject to the norms and sanctions set by laws.
>
> Prevention implies various levels or kinds of action: a priori or primary prevention, the purpose of which is to prevent the violation of norms of behaviour; and a posteriori prevention which comprises the secondary and tertiary, which acts on persons who have already committed offences. Every preventive programme must have these two aspects.
>
> A priori prevention has the advantage of dealing with the problem before its birth. At that stage, it is at the community level that interdisciplinary teams in collaboration with the whole social group ought to be active and play an important role.
>
> Areas calling for priority investigation in the next five years include: drug addiction, means of communication

and family conflicts.

Crime prevention, so far as application of means of social prophylaxis is concerned, depends largely on coordination of all the national services that contribute directly or indirectly to this function of the State.[53]

The preventive anticriminal action which it proposes therefore includes study of personal and social antecedents of criminal acts; establishment of a social prophylaxis plan on the basis of criminological study; training of personnel in preventive methods; community education in prevention; unified statistics; drafting of crime-prevention laws, regulations, and standards; and coordination of all governmental plans related to crime prevention.

c. Inclusion of Crime Control in Insular Investment Plans

The planning system in Puerto Rico deals fully with what it calls "public protection and safety." This is partly because Puerto Rico has geared its planning directly to the budgetary process: each operating agency submits its own sectoral plan, to which the planning board attaches chronological priorities and a four-year timetable, on the strength of which it can recommend to the legislature an appropriation for the next fiscal year. By this process Puerto Rico has kept down its capital budget for crime control facilities to an extraordinarily low level of 1 or 1.5 percent, particularly by postponing improvements in penal institutions until there was a plan for the correctional subsector and by renting police stations instead of constructing them.

---

53. Venezuela, CORDIPLAN, IV *Plan de la Nación, 1970–1974* [Version Preliminar], Vol. 2 (Caracas: El Desarollo Social Cultural, 1970). Translated from the Spanish.

TABLE I
PLANNED INVESTMENT—PUERTO RICO ($1,000,000)

Scope	1963/64	1963/67	1973/74
Nonrecurrent total	101	458	173
Public protection and safety, total	1.5	4.3	40
Police	0.8	0.8	0.2
Law courts	0.3	1.0	0.3
Juvenile delinquency	0.4	2.5	—
Prisons	—	—	3.5

The Puerto Rican Planning Board has written:

Violations of the law have an enormous social cost which may affect particular individuals or society as a whole. Private costs are in the forms of loss of assets of particular individuals, psychic damage to individuals, and partial or total loss of capacity to be gainfully employed. Public costs are involved in the form of resources used to finance the judicial system, the police and the penal system.

Although the total costs of criminal activity have not been estimated, the total costs are undoubtedly greater in the long run than the investment in removing the socio-economic causes of crime.[54]

Barbados also has included in its development plans (1960/65/68) its capital expenditure on prisons, approved schools, and police barracks, keeping these down to less than 1 percent of the total, with the comment:

> The remedial services which formerly went under the general terms of "welfare" . . . were primarily concerned both with helping the individual . . . and in protecting the community from the unsocial behaviour of the individual. These services have of necessity been concerned with cases of social breakdown either through ill-health, family difficulty or delinquency and the emphasis has usually been on an immediate remedy for the individual, e.g. . . . confinement in prison or other corrective institution.
> Provision for such services must of necessity continue to be made, but the aim of the government is to stabilize as far as possible existing institutional facilities and to improve the human resources of the country and the well-being of its people by a constructive approach.[55]

Jamaica included in its independence plan proposed capital expenditure on police, courts, prisons, and juvenile institutions, to a total of just over 1 percent of all planned investment in the public sector.

Trinidad and Tobago, on the other hand, have included in the plan only social welfare investments in congregate care for juveniles.

---

54. Puerto Rico, Planning Board, *Four-Year Economic Programme, 1968 to 1971* (San Juan, 1967).

55. Barbados, *Development Plan, 1960–1965* (Bridgetown, 1960).

d. Place of Crime Control in Recurrent Expenditures

The fear which Latin American planners have of scarce resources being wasted on governmental overheads has resulted in some of their plans including estimates of what they hope may be the declining share of justice and police in total governmental expenditure. In one country this has included a plan to reduce expenditures on justice and police from almost as high a share as that of education or health to only about half of what was planned for these other services (Dominican Republic). The well-known tendency for plans to overestimate investment may be accompanied by a tendency to underestimate recurrent outlays on criminal policy.

2. SECTORAL PLANNING

The three Latin American plans that have recently included sections on justice or social defense have cut across the traditional boundaries between the various organized sub-sectors. Argentina writes of federal police equipment, law reform, improvements in prosecution, new prisons, and the technicalization of corrections (1971/75). Brazil plans for improvements in the federal police, federal law reform, and improvement in the courts of first instance, as well as general emphasis on law and order and internal security (1970). Venezuela gives the criminal justice sector a unified approach as "a posteriori prevention," including community treatment, speeding up of trials, reorientation of correctional personnel, release under supervision, correctional social work, and legalization of open prisons as well as building of new prisons (1970–74).

Puerto Rico uses its annual budget as a means of implementing its four-year plan. It therefore groups all "protection and safety of persons and property" in a single "programmatic area," which includes not only justice, law and order, and custody and rehabilitation but also protection of the citizen as consumer, proprietor, and employee, as well as protection and aid against disasters.

3. SUBSECTORAL PLANNING

a. Law Enforcement
None of the plans as such gives any indication of the size of the police force or the dimensions of the lawbreaking with which it has to deal; but Barbados has planned barracks for 300 police. Dominican (1968–75) and Salvadorean planning appear to be almost alone in indicating the operating cost, and Puerto Rico has not done so regularly.

The Puerto Rican police have had a long-term plan for the construction of their own facilities, because as of 1963 the state owned only 24 of 82 police stations and 13 of 46 outposts; but the Planning Board recommended for the quadrennium only $0.5 million toward the $13.5 million in permanent improvements programmed by the police.

El Salvador's planning covers both "public security" and "national defense," and takes account of their merger since 1962.

It is known from sources other than the plans that there may be considerable diversity in police systems. Some countries are reported to assign army officers and men to police duties (El Salvador, Nicaragua). One is reported to have innovated by instituting a professional police trained to be helpful to rural communities (Costa Rica, *guardia de asistencia rural*). Some have a number of noncoordinated police forces, which impedes unified planning. In some, where public police are supplemented with privately paid plantation agents or urban *serenos*, public policing may represent only part of the cost of policing. In some, the ratio of police to population may seem high, as for example in a small country where there is no army and the rural areas are well policed. In some, police reports may indicate a significant proportion of apprehensions for victimless offenses and breaches of public order. In general, Latin American and Caribbean countries tend to be highly policed.

b. Judicial Planning

The concern of Latin American governments with prison overcrowding has recently led some of them to include in their development plans some proposals for changes in the judicial process. Argentina plans for law reform and improvements in prosecutions (1971). Brazil plans improvements in federal courts, especially of first instance (1970). Venezuela plans the speeding up of trials and more discretion in applying penalties imposed by a court (1970).

Until these recent developments, development plans have referred only to minor construction costs of additional or improved law courts. The capital outlay on law courts was referred to as something too small to mention in detail (Costa Rica, 1965–68), or as amounting to about 3 percent of domestically financed investments (Nicaragua, 1966). In Puerto Rico the judiciary had a plan for 123 units to cost more than $12 million, toward which the Planning Board recommended less than $1 million for one quadrennium (1963/67).

c. Treatment of Offenders

The correctional pattern in Latin America is dominated by custodial institutions, usually under quasi-military discipline, which serve also as places of detention for persons awaiting trial, with the suspended sentence serving as principal alternative to post-sentence imprisonment. The proportion of the population in prison averages about twice as high as in Europe and the proportion of prisoners awaiting trial reaches 75 percent in several countries and is probably the highest in the world. Such planning as refers to corrections tends therefore to set as its main objective the diminution of prison overcrowding by lessening the load of nonsentenced inmates, spreading the prisoners among additional institutions and speeding the exit of prisoners by supervised release until the end of their sentences.

Practical implementation of the Standard Minimum Rules for the Treatment of Prisoners has not been referred to in any planning, although Argentina embodied them in its national prison law (1958), as did Chile in its presidential regulations on fundamental standards for the application of a national prison policy (1965) and Venezuela in its prison system law (1961). Some have also reported a considerable effort through the 1960s to bring actual organization and administration into line with the Rules (e.g., Venezuela).

Puerto Rican planning has included a study of correctional institutions, and formerly stood alone in indicating the dimensions of the prison problem and in proposing priorities. This would seem to be related partly to the nature of its planning, but partly also to an incidence of incarceration as high as that of the continental United States. While the study was proceeding, the Planning Board omitted prison improvements from its capital budget (1963-67). After it was completed $15.5 million was recommended for inclusion in the capital budget for the next quadrennium (1968/72). Part of this was for bringing the capacity of the prisons into line with their work load: in addition to other permanent improvements, provision was recommended for a large youth correctional institution (capacity 600) and three minimum security camps (260 each). Part, however, was directed to:

(i) Minimization of total annual government expenditure on penal policy; and,
(ii) Expansion of rehabilitation programmes which can be self-paying.

One recommendation was therefore for $2 million for a self-balancing prison industries corporation, to enable it to employ or train all the 1,225 sentenced prisoners who were adjudged employable. The other was for $4 million for treatment of over 1,300 addicts who could not otherwise be employed or released on parole. In addition to these objectives, the plan stated its broader principles as follows:

> A comprehensive penal policy must consider all public policies which are directly or indirectly related to violations of the law. This implies that overall educational planning, manpower development and employment planning must be connected with penal planning. Penal planning in turn must be based on the existing and potential educational planning and labour market conditions.
>
> The goals of minimization of unemployment and increasing the quantity and quality of education bear directly on penal policy. Employment status and educational attainments are related to criminal activity . . . . The vast majority of recidivists are unemployed and have less than five years education.[56]

Venezuela's planning for "a posteriori prevention" sets the decongesting of the prisons and the lessening of recidivism as its underlying themes (1970–74). It proposes:

- An Aid in Freedom Service to promote group and community acceptance of ex-prisoners;
- Bolivars 29 million for building new penitentiaries;
- Speeding up of the judicial process to lessen imprisonment of persons awaiting trial;
- Training of prison guards to understand that therapy is more important than intensifying the repressive character of penalties;

---

56. Puerto Rico, Planning Board, *Four-Year Economic Programme, 1968 to 1971* (San Juan, 1970).

- Promotion of supervisors and guards on the basis of demonstrated success in preventing recidivism;
- Supervised release;
- Open prison: experimentation and legalization;
- Correctional social work for individualized rehabilitation and readjustment, both in and after prison, by 1974.

Argentina's plan proposes new prisons, of which one would be for detention of persons awaiting trial, as well as an application of modern techniques to the running of prisons (1971). Brazil is also planning extensive investment in new prisons.

One notes, in a few countries, the beginning of the kind of criminological research that could have an impact on policy planning among a widening range of correctional options. In Chile, for example, controlled experiments have been made in workday and weekend furloughs. In Guyana the interaction is being explored between availability of "fit persons" to supervise probationers, imposition of fines, and imprisonment for non-payment of fines; and the relevance is also being studied of imprisonment for nonsupport in a society where illegitimacy is widespread.[57]

d. Juvenile Delinquency

It is reported that the Inter-American Child Welfare Institute has assisted some governments with comprehensive planning for child protection, including prevention and treatment of delinquency (e.g., Nicaragua). Although there is a widespread

---

57. Cecil N. Murray, "Identifying Social Defence Policy Needs and Research Resources," paper prepared for the Interregional Seminar on the Use of Research as a Basis for Social Defence Policy and Planning, Rungstedgaard, Denmark, 20–30 August 1973.

breakdown of family authority, and most Latin American countries have a national council for the protection of children, it remains nevertheless exceptional for programs for child protection to be included in development plans.[58]

The Puerto Rican Planning Board has included in its capital budget recommendations for permanent improvements in the social welfare institutions of the health department: $2.5 million to include two new reception and observation centers as well as twelve other institutions, which would raise the capacity of juvenile institutions to 1,800 (1963/67), followed by $5 million to add three more to the four existing detention homes as well as three other institutions (1968-72).

The Trinidad and Tobago plan has also included small capital outlays on places of safety for court-detained juveniles, girls' corrective homes, and accommodation for probationers.

D. WESTERN ASIA

1. COMPREHENSIVE PLANNING APPROACHES TO CRIMINAL POLICY

a. Degress of Inclusion or Exclusion in Investment Planning

(i) *Comprehensive inclusion.* There is a widespread tendency in the Arab East to include all aspects of criminal policy among the objects of capital investment under national development plans. In oil-rich and other countries where considerable resources are available for investment in a wide range of developmental facilities, the proportion allocated to crime control may nevertheless appear small. In a country in which the resources available for investment are highly hypothetical or contingent, the proportion projected for crime control may appear even

58. *International Review of Criminal Policy,* No. 21 (1963), pp. 45-54 (United Nations publication, Sales No.: 64.IV.3).

lower.

(ii) *Selective inclusion.* Turkey's development plan has only called attention to the problem of juvenile delinquency (1963–67, 1968–72) or has completely omitted criminal justice (1968–77). Jordan has omitted from its development plan all capital outlay on security and justice while including among its social welfare outlays the small sums required to build additional institutions for delinquent juveniles (1964–70).

(iii) *Omission.* Israel's development plan leaves all details concerning governmental facilities to be filled in later.

Lebanon's outlay on crime control facilities may have reached about 1 percent of public works outlay on the eve of its preplanning studies.[59]

b. Implications for Recurrent Expenses

Jordan planned for a decline in the share of crime control in the recurrent expenses of the central government (see Table II).

TABLE II
PLANNED ANNUAL OUTLAY BY JORDAN

Year	Total Central Expenditure ($1,000,000)	Expenditures on Justice (Police and Juvenile Delinquency)	Ratio of (3) to (2) in %
(1)	(2)	(3)	(4)
1961	JD 28	2.5	9
1964	JD 34.6	2.7	8
1970 (projected)	JD 41	2.7	7

59. Institut de Recherche et de Formation en vue du Développement Harmonisé (Paris, 1961).

2. SECTORAL PLANNING AGAINST CRIME

No country plan in Western Asia provides any evidence of integrated criminal policy planning. It is reported, however, that in Iraq a national center for social research and criminology, in the Ministry of Social Affairs, studies current problems for possible use by the government.

On the other hand, governments in this region have always participated in charity toward the unfortunate. This function is today exercised by ministries of social affairs, which have consequently become influential in a considerable range of preventive and rehabilitative activities, sometimes on behalf of prisoners and always on behalf of the young, including delinquents. Insofar as a ministry of social affairs thinks in social work terms, it tends in this region to become a center for innovative social planning.

This is evident in the probation service developed in Jordan, where the social workers of the Ministry of Social Affairs have been available for court social work and prison aftercare, although it is used more on behalf of juveniles than of adults.

From the planning viewpoint, this trend has two contradictory aspects. On one side, there is an emphasis on services, which does not lend itself to inclusion in a capital expenditure plan, although here they are often included. On the other side, there is a tradition of benevolent foundations investing in buildings. Governmental investment in construction of buildings for a social purpose may be regarded as being in a sense a continuation of this tradition.

Parallel but separate has been a tradition of concentration of power. Thus, "security" in the Kuwaiti plan may be used to cover defense as well as police. Armed forces play an active role in intelligence and surveillance, maintaining order, adjudicating offenses against public authority, and executing penal sanctions against convicted enemies of authority.

3. SUBSECTORAL PLANNING PROBLEMS

a. Law Enforcement

One plan mentions juvenile bureaus in police departments (Turkey, 1968). Iraqi plans have contained considerable investments in police facilities: mobile police barracks, police schools, a police hospital, police office buildings, and police stations. Kuwait has planned housing for police. Syria has included a college for police cadets.

This tends to be a heavily policed region.

b. Judicial Process

Housing for courts and judges has constituted an important item in Iraqi and Syrian plans.

c. Treatment of Offenders

The United Nations Standard Minimum Rules for Treatment of Prisoners are not known to have been translated into Arabic or any other official language of the area. Nor do any development plans suggest a sectoral program for their implementation. Kuwait nevertheless replied to the United Nations request for a periodic report concerning their application (IRCP 26:74). And Iraq is reported to have based its treatment of prisoners law (1969) on these minimum rules.

Nearly half the crime control outlay in Iraqi development plans has been for places of confinement. In addition to local jails and provincial prisons for 250 prisoners of both sexes, these include an immense central prison complex at Abu Ghraib to comprise "wards for prisoners holding 2,088 beds, an arrest hall, an administration section, factories for training prisoners in different professions and crafts, women's and children's centres, a school, a hospital and a mosque." One quarter of the planned crime control investment in Syria has been for prisons.

Turkey has reported education and training for young prisoners, but has noted the lack of aftercare. (1968).

Several plans are also concerned with alternatives to begging. Syria has planned small work homes for beggars and for prostitutes at Damascus and Aleppo. Iraq planned al-Rashad city "to ensure the necessary social cure of the incapacitated, the vagrants and delinquents, through providing them with residential quarters, food, clothing and health care, as well as all necessary means for vocational training and social education and whatever is necessary to prepare these needy people for a full and honourable life and make of them good and productive citizens" (1961); construction was to begin with 100 houses for the officials and employees who would run the project, and then proceed to 183 residential units to shelter 900 citizens.

The custodial character of the penal institutions and the non-professional character of their personnel may sometimes be linked to their being staffed by police or to the low ratio of staff to prisoners (Iraq, 1:19).

d. Juvenile Delinquency

The family structure of this region has always produced a considerable number of homeless boys who go to the cities. At the same time, its traditions of personal charity (*zakat*) and endowed foundations (*awqaf*) have operated in favor of the young, and especially of "orphans." Governments have always participated in this charity and operate today through ministries of social affairs.

Some social affairs planning is preventive and usually includes promotion of homes for homeless children, often to be operated by grant-aided voluntary agencies. Syria, for example, reports nearly 2,000 children in orphanages.

Other social affairs planning is regarded as rehabilitative. Thus Iraqi, Jordanian, Kuwaiti, and Syrian plans have contained small sums for institutions for juvenile delinquents. Syria, with about 600 in juvenile detention centers and reformatories, has included a new reeducation center for girls as well as a second one for boys. Jordan has planned to add to its three remand homes two more for 50 boys each and two for 30 girls each, as well as to open two new reform schools for 50 boys each (in addition to one old one for 100 boys) and one for 50 girls (besides one old one for 20 girls).

Several countries have included in their plans a declaration of intention to change their juvenile protection law. Jordan has planned a new juvenile protection law to improve the condition of children in jails and to set up special children's tribunals. Turkey planned to complete the drafting of a juvenile court law and the preparation for its implementation (1965); but this had not been achieved by the beginning of the next plan period (1968), when it was noted that there were no juvenile courts and no provision for noninstitutional treatment.

Outside their plans, it is reported that some countries in this region have associated a child guidance clinic (Iraq) or social workers and an observation center (Lebanon) with juvenile court social work, or have organized supervised probation (Cyprus, Israel, Jordan); but it is understood that some countries have hesitated to use probation and other alternatives to congregate care, or to empower juvenile courts to vary the treatment prescribed for a juvenile.

CONCLUSIONS

While the purpose of this survey has not been to verify any even preliminary hypothesis, and while due to the nature of the data and the built-in constraints, no rigorous methodology could be followed which would permit definitive conclusions to be drawn, some tentative observations might be made on the basis of the material assembled.

The first thing that strikes even the cursory analyst is that poor countries with less crime are often spending proportionately more on crime than richer countries. This preliminary conclusion—based on what is admittedly incomplete evidence—warrants further study if the implications of all the figures included in the published budgets are to be fully explored and the information given subjected to qualitative analysis. It can be said even at this stage, however, that in terms of national investment crime control has been important, especially in developing countries.

It would seem to follow that a country's development planning and the technical cooperation required by it might well pay more attention to a governmental activity that appears to be exceptionally sensitive to the disruption of customary ways of living and to rapid changes in people's standards and opportunities.

This would appear to be equally valid, both in comprehensive planning and in the planning of the criminal policy sector itself.

In the crime control sector there is room for increased exchange of information and experience among policymakers and practitioners, linked to the promotion of systemic thinking about criminal justice, so as to better understand and modify the interfacing of the various subsectors.

From a theoretical viewpoint, the challenge to further study, both internationally and nationally, is equally clear.

The aggregative data connected with planning or financing a government's crime control activities do not seem to show much, if any, obvious and simple correlation with per capita income, years of schooling, life expectancy, age grouping, urbanization, or other quantifiable indicators of levels of living. It is possible that detailed breakdowns, insofar as they have been made, might be more revealing. It would also seem possible that the significance of crime control planning and budgeting data might be sought in their relationship to hard-to-quantify institutional variables. It is to be hoped, therefore, that this very preliminary survey may help stimulate comparative research along these difficult lines.

Appendix 1

Note on Method

This survey does not set out from a theoretical hypothesis to be assayed according to a preformulated methodology. Instead, it merely roots out and assembles much hitherto scattered administrative data.

In an essentially administrative survey of a field of governmental action in which there is no standardized international reporting, it has been necessary to accept each country's own definitions of crime control. As far as possible, even the country's terminology has been kept, so that the reference may be to "maintenance of internal security," to "law and order," to "police and justice," to "criminal justice," in some to certain "expenses of sovereignty," and in yet others to a mere listing of police, courts, and prisons.

Private outlay on protection has been excluded, since it is always unplanned and often unreported, although it is well known that in most countries and in both rural and urban areas government has no monopoly in this field of action.

The military have posed a difficult problem of classification. On the one hand, they may constitute an internal security force, in all countries to some degree, and in developing countries to a major extent. On the other hand, they may essentially symbolize the sovereignty, unity, and integrity of the state. It is impossible to determine to what extent each of these two functions contributes to the tendency for the military to be more heavily armed and better equipped than the police, with all that this implies for the allocation of investment capital, budgetary outlays, and foreign resources. Their inclusion would frequently have

95

doubled the estimate of a country's allocation of fiscal resources to internal security. Armed forces other than the gendarmerie have nevertheless been omitted in order not to exaggerate governmental outlay on security and so as to focus on those internal security services of which a certain degree of technical crime control competence, day in and day out, is to be expected, especially since United Nations aid has been more normally available at a government's request for technical cooperation with civilian than with military services.

A social scientist might study an internal security apparatus as an income-transfer, power-distribution, and value-allocation output of a political system. It would appear, however, that the United Nations, under its charter obligation to promote economic and social development and progress in larger freedom, is concerned with the *definition and containment of lawbreaking primarily as a means of promoting higher levels of living and respect for human rights.* The basic purpose of this United Nations survey is therefore not to construct an abstract behavioral model—although it might be useful if an appropriate research institute were to attempt to do so—but to review the method and extent of governmental planning of crime control for internationally recognized purposes.

The method followed in this administrative survey is to look at four dimensions of criminal justice—referred to in the report as subsectors or subsystems, in view of their tendency to separate organization—and within each to look at those variables that have been taken into account.

The task has been complicated by the fact that quantitative indicators useful for this purpose are largely lacking. In particular, it has not been possible to use the old established and widely produced statistics recording the quantity of work done by the various crime control agencies in moving offenders through the system, e.g., the offenses recorded by the police, the offenses they solve, the cases judged and offenders sentenced by the courts, the offenders received into and discharged from institutions or probation in the course of a year. These series of "crime statistics" were originally initiated in order to see what effect the criminal law reforms of the early nineteenth century were having on the incidence of crime; they have proved useful to the various crime control agencies as a means of influencing public opinion and legislatures; and they have been used critically by sociologists of crime and of criminal law. They are hard to use comparatively between different countries or periods, because of the varying and subjective element that enters into the recording of offenses by officials, e.g., crimes of serious violence may increase if what was reported as "hitting" yesterday is reported as "wounding" today; the uncertain degree to which victims report property loss or damage; and the incompleteness with which public officials take cognizance of victimless offenses.[60]

Instead, four quantitative indicators of administrative resource allocation have been used in order to give some rough measure of the order of magnitude involved:

(a) Multi-year investment plans, supplemented in some countries by annual capital budgets, provide a rough indication of hoped-for outlay on physical facilities or fixed assets, although underspending is common.

(b) Recurrent operating expenditure is sometimes forecast in a multiyear investment plan, but is more frequently obtainable from budgetary estimates or reports of expenditure. So far as possible these expenditure figures are net of capital outlay and

---

60. For a discussion of some of the limitations of criminal statistics, see "Organization of Research for Policy Development in Social Defence," working paper prepared by the Secretariat for the Fourth United Nations Congress on the Prevention of Crime and the Treatment of Offenders, (A/CONF.43/4), pages 7-13.

net after deduction of earnings (fines, proceeds from sale of prison produce, etc.).

(c) The size of police force is frequently given in an investment plan, often in an annual budget, and most often in an annual administrative report from which it is copied in a statistical yearbook. As far as possible, actual police strength is cited, but in some cases this may include clerical and mechanical workers in police departments, and in some the available data may not distinguish between actual strength and a slightly larger authorized or budgeted establishment.

(d) The number of persons in prison is derived as far as possible from information which has been communicated to the United Nations Secretariat by forty-three cooperating governments and relates to 1 December 1972. It is supplemented from other official published reports, relating usually to the last day of the fiscal or calendar year, but less frequently to average daily occupancy. Reports do not always make clear to what extent national data include prisoners in local jails, or awaiting trial, or detained without trial, or civil prisoners.

Appendix 2
Supporting Tables

ANNUAL COST OF CRIME CONTROL OPERATIONS
PERCENTAGE OF ANNUAL RECURRENT BUDGETED EXPENDITURES

AFRICA	ASIA AND FAR EAST	AMERICAS	WESTERN ASIA
20 Lesotho			
17 Ethiopia			
16 Sierra Leone			
15 Somalia			
14 Kenya			
		13 Colombia	
12.5 Uganda	12 Hong Kong		
	11 South Korea	11 Chile	
10.0 Algeria		Guyana	
Botswana		10 Dominican Republic	
Benin		Panama	
Ivory Coast		9 Jamaica	9 Cyprus
Madagascar			
Morocco			8.5 Kuwait
Swaziland		8 Barbados	
Togo	8 Iran	El Salvador	
9.0 Malawi	7.5 Philippines	Puerto Rico	7 Jordan
Rhodesia	7 Afghanistan		
Tunisia	Indonesia		
8.0 Egypt	6.5 Laos	6 Bolivia	
Mauritius	Malaysia	Brazil	
7.0 Gambia	Thailand		5 Lebanon
6.0 Ghana	6 India		
Nigeria	Pakistan		
S. Africa	5.5 Fiji		4 Turkey
Zaire	4.5 Singapore	4.5 Venezuela	
5.0 Senegal	4 Sri Lanka	4. Costa Rica	
Zambia	3 Australia	Ecuador	3 Iraq
4.0 Malta	Japan	3 Nicaragua	Israel
	2 New Zealand	U.S.A.	Syria

100

POLICE
RATE PER 1,000 POPULATION

	AFRICA	ASIA AND FAR EAST	AMERICAS	WESTERN ASIA
4	4.2 Malta	4.0 Singapore	5.6 Bahamas	11.7 Bahrain
				4.0 Israel
				3.5 Cyprus
3		3.0 Hong Kong	3.0 Barbados, Costa Rica	3.0 Jordan 2.9 Iraq
			2.7 Puerto Rico	
			2.5 Trinidad	
	2.2 Mauritius	2.2 Thailand	2.3 Chile	
2	2.0 Ghana Kenya Somalia Swaziland	2.0 Fiji	2.0 Colombia	
			1.8 Canada	
	1.6 S.Africa 1.5 Botswana 1.4 Ethiopia	1.7 Australia Japan 1.5 Taiwan 1.4 Korea 1.2 India 1.1 New Zealand	1.6 Jamaica	
	1.1 Uganda Sierra Leone			
1	1.0 Madagascar Zaire		0.9 Brazil	
	0.7 Egypt Tanzania		0.5 Guyana	
	0.5 Nigeria			

PRISONERS
RATE PER 100,000 POPULATION

	AFRICA	ASIA AND FAR EAST	EUROPE	AMERICAS	WESTERN ASIA
400	South Africa				
300	Swaziland				
250	Lesotho			Bahamas	
230	Kenya				
200				U.S.A.	
180		Fr. Polynesia		Colombia / El Salvador	
170				Costa Rica	Turkey
160	Uganda				
150	Sierra Leone	Hong Kong			
140	Botswana				Israel
130		Australia / Thailand		Panama / Venezuela	
120	Ivory Coast / Tunisia			Guyana / Jamaica / Trinidad	Lebanon
110		Singapore / Taiwan			
101			Finland		
100	Ghana / Morocco	Fiji		Argentina / Canada / Chile	
94			United Kingdom		
90		New Zealand		Mexico	
87			West Germany		
80	Angola / Egypt / Ethiopia	Korea / Sri Lanka		Ecuador	
71			Denmark		
70		Indonesia			Jordan
64			Belgium		
63			France		
60	Malta	Pakistan / Burma			Iraq
55			Italy		
54			Sweden		
50		Iran / Japan / Philippines		Barbados	
40					Syria
37			Ireland		
30		India			Cyprus
21			Netherlands		

APPENDIX 2

TABLE 1

PLANNED CAPITAL INVESTMENT ON CRIME CONTROL IN AFRICA

Country	Plan Period	Total Planned Capital Outlay on Public Sector (in millions)	Planned Capital Outlay on Crime Control (in millions)	Ratio of (4) to (3) %	Notes on (4)
(1)	(2)	(3)	(4)	(5)	(6)
Swaziland	1969–70	R 2	R 0.2	10	
	1969–74	R 23	R 0.2	5.6	
	1973–77	R 42	R 1.0	2.5	
Liberia	1971	$ 8.8	$ 0.8	9.9	Annual Development Budget
Uganda	1966/71	Sh 1,800	Sh 207	12.0	
	1971/71	Sh 2,600	Sh 244	9.4	
Zambia	1965–66	£ 35	£ 2	5.5	
	1966–70	£ 282	£ 6.5		
Lesotho	1970–75	R 28	R 1.3	4.5	
Sudan	1961–71	S £ 90	S £ 4	4.4	
Central African Rep.	1965–66	CAF Fr 6725	CAF Fr 275	4	Omits prisons, courts
Ghana	1951–58	G £ 118	G £ 3	2.5	
	1959–64	G £ 250	G £ 8.4	3.6	2.5% if hydroelectric works included in (3)
	1963/70	G £ 476	G £ 5.8	1.2	
Kenya	1965–70	K £ 87	K £ 2.1	3.4	
	1970–74	K £ 192	K £ 5	2.5	
Nigeria	1962–68	£ 677	£ 11	1.7	Actually spent: £ 8
	1970–74	£ 780	£ 18	2.5	

TABLE 1 (Cont.)

PLANNED CAPITAL INVESTMENT ON CRIME
CONTROL IN AFRICA

Country	Plan Period	Total Planned Capital Outlay on Public Sector (in millions)	Planned Capital Outlay on Crime Control (in millions)	Ratio of (4) to to (3) %	Notes on (4)
(1)	(2)	(3)	(4)	(5)	(6)
Tanzania	1964–69	£ 246	£ 3	1.2	Not including Air Wing support and National Service Training
	1969–74	Sh 2750	Sh 75	2.7	
Gambia	1967/71	£ 5	£ 0.11	2.2	
Mauritania	1963/66	CFA Fr 13,500	CFA Fr 300	2.2	Includes gendarmerie
	1970/73	CFA Fr 47,000	CFA Fr 900	2.0 Gendarmerie only	
Morocco	1960–64	Frs 259,000	Frs 2340	1.0	Omits juveniles
	1968–72	DH 5,000	DH 110	2.2	
	1968/69	DH 1,200	DH 65	5.0	Regular budget investments
Togo	1966/70	CFA Fr 20,050	CFA Fr 439	2.2	Includes gendarmerie

104

TABLE 1 (Cont.)
PLANNED CAPITAL INVESTMENT ON CRIME
CONTROL IN AFRICA

Country	Plan Period	Total Planned Capital Outlay on Public Sector (in millions)	Planned Capital Outlay on Crime Control (in millions)	Ratio of (4) to to (3) %	Notes on (4)
(1)	(2)	(3)	(4)	(5)	(6)
Mauritius	1960–66	R 400	Rs 3.6	0.9	
	1966–70	R 337	Rs 7.2	2.1	
Rhodesia	1965–68	£ 82	£ 1.7	2	
Guinea	1960–63	Frs. 38,912	Frs. 695	1.8	
Ivory Coast	1960–70	CFA Fr 170,000	CFA Fr 4500	1.5	
Botswana	1968–73	R 70	R 0.63	0.9	
	1970–75	R 95	R 0.3	0.3	
Egypt	1960–65	E 4 1170	E £ 85	0.7	
Benin	1966–70	CFA Fr 25,640	CFA Fr 160	0.6	Includes gendarmerie
Algeria	1967	AD 1672	AD 4	0.2	Capital budget
Senegal	1969–73	CFA Fr 125,000	CFA Fr 250	0.2	Includes gendarmerie
Ethiopia	1963–67	Eth $1696	E $3.6	. . .	For children only
Somalia	1963–68	So. Sh. 1400	S. Sh. 1	. . .	For children only
	1968–70	So. Sh. 700	. . .	. . .	Plan omits governmental overheads

TABLE 2

RECURRENT EXPENDITURE ON CRIME CONTROL AS A PROPOR-
TION OF TOTAL GOVERNMENTAL OPERATING EXPENSES IN
AFRICA

Lesotho	Plan (1970/75): 17.5 percent gross or 16 percent net Budget (1971): 20 percent
Ethiopia	Budget (1970): 17 percent
Sierra Leone	Budget (1971): 16 percent
Somalia	Plan (1961,1968): 15 percent
Kenya	Budget (1973): 16 percent
Uganda	Budget (1972): 12.5 percent
Algeria	Budget (1966): 10 percent
Botswana	Plan (1974/75): 10 percent
Benin	Plan (1966/70): 10 percent
Ivory Coast	Plan (1960/70): 10 percent
Malagasy Republic	Plan (1960/70): 10 percent
Morocco	Budget (1969): 10 percent (half of Justice and In- terior)

TABLE 2 (Cont.)

RECURRENT EXPENDITURE ON CRIME CONTROL AS A PROPORTION OF TOTAL GOVERNMENTAL OPERATING EXPENSES IN AFRICA

Swaziland	Budget (1971): 10 percent
Togo	Plan (1966/70): 10 percent
Malawi	Budget (1971): 9 percent
Rhodesia	Budget (1971): 9 percent
Tunisia	Budget (1969): 9 percent
Egypt	Plan (1960/65): 8 percent
Mauritius	Budget (1971): 8 percent
Gambia	Plan (1967/71): 7 percent
Ghana	Budget (1969): 6 percent
Nigeria	Budget (1969): 6 percent
South Africa	Budget (1974): 6 percent
Zaire	Budget (1973): 6 percent
Senegal	Budget (1970): 5 percent
Zambia	Budget (1971): 5 percent
Malta	Budget (1970): 4 percent

TABLE 3

POLICE FORCES IN AFRICAN COUNTRIES

Country	Year	Strength	Ratio to 1,000 Population	Notes
(1)	(2)	(3)	(4)	(5)
Malta	1969	1,385	4.2	
Mauritius	1966	1,650	2.2	Authorized 1,875 (2.5)
Somalia	1971	7,000	2.0	
Kenya	1973	22,500	2.0	Budgeted
Ghana[a]	1970	18,600	2.0	Authorized 19,935
Swaziland	1973	750	2.0	Authorized Planned 880
Zambia	1970	7,500	1.8	
South Africa	1973	34,517	1.6	Budgeted 35,221 (1974)
Botswana	1970	1,090	1.5	Authorized Planned 1,265 (1975)
Ethiopia	1970	34,000	1.4	Authorized 40,000 (17)

[a]E. Lefever, *Spear and Scepter* (Washington, D.C.: Brookings Institution, 1970).

APPENDIX 2

TABLE 3 (Cont.)

POLICE FORCES IN AFRICAN COUNTRIES

Country	Year	Strength	Ratio to 1,000 Population	Notes
(1)	(2)	(3)	(4)	(5)
Uganda[b]	1972	10,000	1.1	Authorized. Actual 6,600 (1968); 0.8 (1971). Planned 1.7 (1981)
Sierra Leone	1971	2,750	1.1	Budgeted. Plus chiefdom police. Census 3,850 or 1.6 (1963)
Zaire	1970	20,000	1.0	
Malagasy Republic	1970	7,000	1.0	Includes gendarmerie
Egypt	1960	175,000	0.7	Security and justice. Planned 186,000 (1965)
Tanzania[c]	1971	10,100	0.7	
Ivory Coast	1970	2,560	0.5	Planned. Gendarmerie only
Nigeria	1972	30,000	0.5	

[b]Social Defence in Uganda, Rome: U.N. Social Defence Research Institute, 1971.
[c]The Nationalist, Dar-es-Salaam, 16 July 1971.

TABLE 4

PRISONERS IN AFRICA*

Country	Year	Occupancy	Ratio to 1,000 Pop.	Awaiting Trial (% in parentheses)	Notes
(1)	(2)	(3)	(4)	(5)	(6)
South Africa	1973	94,000	4.0	16,000 (17)	—
Swaziland	1973	1,350	3.0	. . .	Capacity 1,700
Lesotho	1970	2,300	2.5	. . .	—
Kenya	1972	19,924	2.3	2,907 (14)	—
Uganda	1970	15,000	1.6	6,575 (30)	Capacity 9,700 Plan 12,700
Sierra Leone	1966	3,000	1.5	. . .	—
Botswana	1971	800	1.4	. . .	Sentenced only. Capacity 600 (1970). Goal 1,000 (1979)
Ivory Coast[a]	1972	5,895	1.2	3,805(65)	

*Based on latest official figures available to the United Nations and citing also earlier figures where there has been a significant change.

[a]Compare: V. D. Du Bois, "Crime and Treatment of the Criminal in Ivory Coast," *American Universities Fieldstaff Reports, West African Series*, 11(1), 1968.

TABLE 4 (Cont.)

PRISONERS IN AFRICA

Country	Year	Occupancy	Ratio to 1,000 Pop.	Awaiting Trial (% in parentheses)	Notes
(1)	(2)	(3)	(4)	(5)	(6)
Tunisia[b]	1972	5,559	1.2	1,526(28)	
Namibia	1971[c]	...	1.0	...	Capacity 725, central prison only
Ghana	1967	7,800	1.0	...	Plus detainees 450. Non-committed 1,500
Morocco	1972	14,434	1.0	7,812(54)	—
Tanzania	1962[e]	10,108	1.0	(21)	
Angola	1969	4,300	0.8	...	—
Egypt	1964[d]	24,000	0.8	3,250 (13)	—

[b]Compare: Abdelwahat Bouhdiba, *Criminalité et changements sociaux en Tunisie,* Tunis, 1965.

[c]*New York Times,* 26 June 1971.

[d]M. Lopez-Rey, *Crime: An Analytical Appraisal* (London, 1970); compare Ahmad Khalifa in A. Milner, ed., *African Penal Systems* (London, 1969): 39, 672 (1.3)

[e]A. Milner, ed., *African Penal Systems* (London, 1969).

111

TABLE 4 (Cont.)

PRISONERS IN AFRICA

Country	Year	Occupancy	Ratio to 1,000 Pop.	Awaiting Trial (% in parentheses)	Notes
(1)	(2)	(3)	(4)	(5)	(6)
Ethiopia	1970	24,500	0.8	8,500(35)	—
Malta	1969	177	0.6	67(35)	—
Nigeria	1965[f]	18,000	0.3	8,500(47)	Plus inmates of local prisons

---

[f]T. O. Elias, ed., *Prison System in Nigeria, (Lagos, 1968)* and *Nigerian Prison System* (1970). A. Milner, *Nigerian Penal System* (London, 1972).

TABLE 5

PLANNED CAPITAL INVESTMENT ON CRIME CONTROL
IN ASIA AND THE FAR EAST

Country	Plan Period	Public Sector		Crime Control		Ratio (4) to (3)
		(in millions)		(in millions)		(%)
(1)	(2)	(3)		(4)		(5)
Burma	1961/65	K	2,630	K	78	3.5
	1965/66[a]	K	258	K	18	7.1
Malaysia	1961/65	M$	2,110	M$	90	3.0
	1966/70	M$	4,550	M$	171	4.0
Fiji	1971/75	$	75	$	2	2.6
	Revised	$	110	$	4	4
Philippines	1971/74	P	3,730	P	16	0.5
Hong Kong	1972/73[b]	$	1,190	$	43	3.5
Singapore	1972/73[b]	M$	343	$	8.5	2.5

[a]Capital budget, home and judicial affairs
[b]Annual budget

TABLE 6

RECURRENT EXPENDITURES ON CRIME CONTROL AS A PROPOR-
TION OF TOTAL GOVERNMENTAL OPERATING EXPENSES IN ASIA
AND THE FAR EAST

Country	Year	Percentage
(1)	(2)	(3)
Hong Kong	Budget 1973	12
Korea (South)	Budget 1971	11
Iran	Plan 1971–74	10
	Budget 1973	8
Philippines	Five- year budget 1968	7.5
Afghanistan	Plan 1967–71	7
Indonesia	Budget 1965	7
Laos	Budget 1969	7
Malaysia	Budget 1973	6.5

TABLE 6 (Cont.)

RECURRENT EXPENDITURES ON CRIME CONTROL AS A PROPOR-
TION OF TOTAL GOVERNMENTAL OPERATING EXPENSES IN ASIA
AND THE FAR EAST

Country	Year	Percentage
(1)	(2)	(3)
Thailand	Budget 1971	6.5
India	Budget 1969	6
Pakistan	Budget 1969	6
Fiji	Budget 1971	5.5
Singapore	Budget 1973	4.5
Sri Lanka	Budget 1973	4
Australia	Budget 1971	3
Japan	Budget 1971	3
New Zealand	Budget 1974	2

TABLE 7

POLICE FORCES IN ASIA AND THE FAR EAST

Country	Date	Strength	Ratio to 1,000 Population	Notes to (3)
(1)	(2)	(3)	(4)	(5)
Singapore	1973	10,000	4.0	Budgeted establishment, Plus 9,400 special constables
Hong Kong	1971	12,500	3.0	Authorized: 14,800 (3.5)
Thailand	1969	76,321	2.2	
Fiji	1973	1,100	2.0	Budgeted establishment
Australia	1971	22,000	1.7	Plus 3,000 other personnel
Japan	1971	185,000	1.7	Plus 25,318 other personnel
Taiwan	1967	20,000	1.5	Regular only
Korea	1971	45,800	1.4	Includes firemen
India	1968	640,000	1.2	Authorized. Plus village watchmen
New Zealand	1970	3,200	1.1	
Sri Lanka	1968	10,550	0.9	
Iran	1968	20,000	0.7	Urban police; rural gendarmerie
Indonesia	1963	69,000	0.7	

TABLE 8

PRISONERS IN ASIA AND THE FAR EAST*

Country	Year	Occupancy	Ratio to 1,000 Population	Awaiting Trial (% in parentheses)	Notes
(1)	(2)	(3)	(4)	(5)	(6)
French Polynesia	1970	150	1.5	25(17)	—
Hong Kong	1970	6,000	1.5	480(8)	—
Singapore	1971	2,321	1.1	112(5)	Plus 824 detained
Australia	1972	16,615	1.3	1,198(7)	—
Thailand	1972	47,857	1.3	. . .	Capacity 34,146. Untried 2,644 (7%) in 1969
Taiwan	1964[a]	13,000	1.1	. . .	—
Fiji	1969	580	1.0	. . .	Target 670 including remand 210 (1970)
New Zeland	1972	2,465	0.9	97(4)	—
Korea (South)	1971	3,000	0.8	. . .	—
Sri Lanka	1972	8,309	0.8	5,135(62)	—
Indonesia	1964	102,000	1.0	6,300(6)	—
	1965	71,000	0.7	2,300(7)	—
Pakistan	1964[a]	32,000	0.7	. . .	
Burma	1965	15,000	0.6	7,000(47)	—
Iran	1970	15,000	0.5	7,500(50)	
Japan	1950	103,000	1.2	. . .	Capacity 65,000
	1960	72,000	0.6	10,500(15)	—
	1965	63,000	0.5	10,000(16)	—
	1972	69,241	0.5	8,390(17)	—

TABLE 8 (Cont.)

PRISONERS IN ASIA AND THE FAR EAST*

Country	Year	Occupancy	Ratio to 1,000 Population	Awaiting Trial (% in parentheses)	Notes
(1)	(2)	(3)	(4)	(5)	(6)
Philippines	1963[a]	23,000	0.8	. . .	National
	1968[b]	19,000	0.5	. . .	15,000
	1970	20,850	0.5	. . .	provincial 5,600 municipal 2,400
Laos	1970	560	0.2	. . .	—
	1972	1,195	0.4	383(32)	—
Viet Nam	1970	6,133	0.4	4,750(80)	—
India	1972	200,000	0.3	. . .	Incomplete
Malaysia	1971	4,047	0.4	. . .	Plus 1,500 detainees
	1972	2,703	0.3	530(20)	—
Khmer Republic	1972	544	0.1	383(32)	—

[a]UN/TAO/AFE/ 14 (1965)
[b]Laurel report to Senate.

118

TABLE 9

PLANNED INVESTMENT IN CRIME CONTROL IN CARIBBEAN
ISLANDS

Country	Plan Years	Public Sector Total (in millions)	Crime Control (in millions)	Ratio (4) to (3) %
(1)	(2)	(3)	(4)	(5)
Jamaica	1963/68	£ 55	£0.6	1.1
Puerto Rico	1963/67	US$458	US$4.3	1.0
	1973/74	173	6.0	2.5
Barbados	1965/68	$ 41	$0.3	0.7
Trinidad and Tobago	1969/73	$380	$0.3[a]	0.1[a]

---

[a] Juvenile delinquency only.

TABLE 10

RECURRENT EXPENDITURES ON GOVERNMENT AND CRIME CONTROL IN LATIN AMERICAN AND CARIBBEAN PLANS AND BUDGETS

Country	Year	Total Government outlay (in millions)	Justice and and police (in millions)		Notes
(1)	(2)	(3)	(4)	(5)	(6)
Colombia	1963	Pesos Col. 4,175	580	13.9	
	1967	6,400	850	13.2	Police 500; Security 50; Justice 270; Ministerio público 30
Haiti	1971	US$ 31	US$ 4	13.0	Half of security budget
Dominican	1964	RD$ 243	RD$ 26	10.7	
Republic	1967	236	17.3	7.3	Projected. Interior and police 13.9; judiciary 3.4
	1969	230	29	12.6	Interior and police 25.6
	1970	340	24.1	7.1	Planned. Interior and police 19
	1971	264	27	10.1	Budgeted. Interior and police only
El Salvador	1961	Colones 116	14	12.0	
	1968	193	17	9.0	Estimated
	1970	242	20	8.3	Planned. Justice 6; public security 7; judiciary 6; fiscalia 1
Guyana	1971	$ 130	14	11.0	Police 9

120

TABLE 10 (Cont.)

RECURRENT EXPENDITURES ON GOVERNMENT AND CRIME CON-
TROL IN LATIN AMERICAN AND CARIBBEAN PLANS AND BUDGETS

Country	Year	Total Government outlay (in millions)	Justice and police (in millions)	Ratio (4) to (3) in %	Notes
(1)	(2)	(3)	(4)	(5)	(6)
Chile	1967	Escudos 4500	480	10.6	Interior 366; justice 80; judiciary 33
Jamaica	1972	$ 184	16.5	9.0	
Panama	1972	130	13	10.0	
Barbados	1965	WI$ 31	2.6	8.0	
Puerto Rico	1973/74	$1400	118	8.0	Column 3 omits Federal outlays
Bolivia	1964	871	55	6.3	
Brazil	1967	Cr 14,000	900	6.3	
Venezuela	1963	Bolivares 5,466	323	6	
	1966	6,301	379	6	Planned
	1963/66	23,500	1,392	5.9	Planned. Central 640; local 752. Ratio 5.7% of central, 18.5% of local expenditures.
	1971	16,000	675	4.5	Expended; central 505; local 170
Costa Rica	1971	Colones 1,247	54	4.3	Budgeted
Ecuador	1970	$ 6,060	240	3.9	Police 140; courts 44
Nicaragua	1960	Córdobas 430	12.2	2.8	
	1965	977	34.1	3.5	
	1969	1,388	43.7	3.2	

TABLE 11

POLICE FORCES IN LATIN AMERICAN
AND CARIBBEAN COUNTRIES

Country	Year	Strength	Ratio to 1,000 Population	Notes
(1)	(2)	(3)	(4)	(5)
Bahamas	1971	948	5.6	—
Barbados	1965	730	3.0	—
Costa Rica	1970	5,550	3.0	—
Puerto Rico	1973	7,500	2.7	Budgeted strength
Trinidad	1970	2,500	2.5	
Chile	1969	23,000	2.3	—
Colombia	1967	40,000	2.0	—
Jamaica	1969	3,100	1.6	Plus district con- stables. Subse- quently 4,000.
Brazil	1969	80,000	0.9	—
Guyana	1969	300	0.5	—

APPENDIX 2

TABLE 12

PRISONERS IN LATIN AMERICAN AND CARIBBEAN COUNTRIES

Country	Year	Occupancy	Ratio to 1,000 Pop.	Awaiting Trial (%)	Notes
(1)	(2)	(3)	(4)	(5)	(6)
Bahamas	1970	. . .	2.5	. . .	Capacity: 434
Colombia	1966ᵃ	32,000	1.8	25,000(78)	Plus 6,600 juveniles
	1972	32,505	1.8	24,262(75)	
El Salvador	1973	6,473	1.8	4,249(66)	—
Costa Rica	1970	27,000	1.7	1,150(43)	Capacity: 2,200
Panama	1972	1,860	1.3	918(49)	
Venezuela	1967	14,540	1.4	9,300(64)	
	1972	13,920	1.3	10,428(75)	
Guyana	1969	880	1.2	131(15)	
Jamaica	1972	2,330	1.2	271(12)	Plus juveniles. Plus 1,500 on probation.
Trinidad	1972	1,112	1.2	173(16)	
Argentina	1972	26,036	1.1	17,972(76)	—
Chile	1964ᵃ	10,757	1.3	5,452(51)	
	1972	9,505ᵇ	1.1	4,204(48)	
Mexico	1972	29,516	0.9	17,573(40)	
Equador	1972	3,705	0.8	1,150(30)	
Barbados	1969	148	0.6	. . .	—
Brazil	1972	(28,538)	(0.3)	. . .	Federal only. Condemned only.

ᵃLópez-Rey, *Crime: An Analytical Appraisal,* (New York, Praeger, 1970).
ᵇReported as of 1 December; 12,458 at 31 December (U.N. Copenhagen seminar, 1973).

TABLE 13

PLANNED CAPITAL INVESTMENT
ON CRIME CONTROL IN WESTERN ASIA

Country	Year	Public Sector (Millions)	Crime Control (Millions)	Ratio of (4) to (3) %
(1)	(2)	(3)	(4)	(5)
Kuwait	1967/72	KD. 507	12.0	2.4
Iraq	1961/66	ID. 566	5.3	1.0
	1965/70	ID. 668	7.7	1.15
Syria	1966/70	S£.3454	4.8	0.15
Egypt	1960/65	E£1170	8.5	0.7
	1971/75	E£.3496	19.0	0.5

APPENDIX 2

TABLE 14

RECURRENT EXPENDITURE ON CRIME CONTROL AS A PROPORTION OF TOTAL GOVERNMENTAL OPERATING EXPENSES IN WESTERN ASIA

Country	Year	Percentage
(1)	(2)	(3)
Cyprus	Budget (1970):	9 (Justice and Police)
Kuwait	Budget (1971):	8.5
Jordan	Plan (1970):	7
Lebanon	Budget (1970):	5 (half of Interior and Justice)
Turkey	Budget (1970):	4
Iraq	Ordinary budget (1971):	3
Syria	Budget (1971):	3
Israel	Ordinary budget (1973):	2.2 (Justice and Police)

TABLE 15

POLICE FORCES IN WESTERN ASIA

Country	Date	Strength	Ratio to 1,000 Population	Note
(1)	(2)	(3)	(4)	(5)
Bahrain	1968	2,330	11.7	
Israel	1965	7,775	3.3	Plus office staff 257
	1971	11,852	4.0	Plus office staff 480, plus prison guards 1,461
Cyprus	1960	2,000	3.5	Authorized police, gendarmerie
Jordan	1961	5,110	3.0	Plus 3,500 guards
Iraq	1969	26,970	2.9	

TABLE 16

PRISONERS IN WESTERN ASIA

Country	Year	Occupancy	Ratio to 1,000 Population	Awaiting Trial (%)
(1)	(2)	(3)	(4)	(5)
Turkey	1969	50,000	1.7	27,000(54)
Israel	1972	4,264	1.4	679(15)
Lebanon	1972	3,554	1.2	1,580(44)
Jordan	1965[a]	1,400	1.2	500(35)
Iraq	1965	8,100	1.0	. . .
	1972	5,931	0.6	3,529(60)
Syria	1965[a]	4,000	0.7	1,600(40)
	1972	2,328	0.4	1,859(81)
Cyprus	1969	260	0.4	. . .
	1972	181	0.3	9(5)

---

[a]Manuel López-Rey, *Crime: An Analytical Appraisal,* (New York, Praeger, 1970).

Index

76, 82-83, 91, 101, 108-109, 116, 122, 126
Positivism, 8-9, 78
Prevention of crime, 8-9, 15, 17, 28, 78, 86, 92
Prison farms, 49-51
Prison labor, 26, 46-51, 85
Probation, supervised, 53-54, 70, 71, 76
Procurator (prosecutor), 17
Prostitution, 17, 21, 68, 92
Restitution, 40, 47
Social affairs (social welfare), ministry, 29, 53, 57-60, 62, 90
Social defense, 7–9, 11, 57-58, 62, 77-79
Social work, correctional, 46, 70, 82, 87, 90, 93
State, sovereign, 15, 21
System, 13, 15, 61, 62
Treatment of offenders, 2, 15-17, 25-29, 43-51, 62, 66-73, 84-87, 91-97, 110-112, 117-118, 123, 127
Treatment in freedom, 16, 24, 26,

29, 53
Tribunals, family, 29, 76, 93; military, 66, 90; popular, 24, 65
Urbanization, 3, 12
United Nations: Asia and Far East Institute, 61, 62, 64, 71, 72, 76; Congresses on Prevention of Crime and Treatment of Offenders, v, 10, 11, 13, 19, 69, 76, 97; Convention, 68; International Review of Criminal Policy, 25, 27, 47, 53, 64, 68, 87, 96, 123; Resolutions, General Assembly, vi, 9, 28; Economic and Social Council, xi; Standard Minimum Rules for Treatment of Prisoners, 27, 43, 67, 85, 91; Technical assistance, 18, 27, 47, 53, 64, 68, 87, 96, 123
Utilitarianism, 15
Village communities, 21, 65
Volunteers, 29, 64, 71
Youth service, 35

DATE DUE

2080